Reading the changes

D1418088

RETHINKING READING

Series Editor: L. John Chapman
School of Education, The Open University

Reading the changes

ELEANOR ANDERSON

Open University Press
Buckingham · *Philadelphia*

Open University Press
Celtic Court
22 Ballmoor
Buckingham
MK18 1XW

and
1900 Frost Road, Suite 101
Bristol, PA 19007, USA

First Published 1992

A catalogue record of this book is available
from the British Library

Library of Congress Cataloging-in-Publication Data

Anderson, Eleanor, 1941–
    Reading the changes / Eleanor Anderson.
        p.   cm. — (Rethinking reading)
    Includes bibliographical references (p.   ) and index.
    ISBN 0-335-15643-6   ISBN 0-335-15642-8 (pbk)
    1. Reading—Great Britain.   I. Title.   II. Series.
LB1050.A47   1992
428.4—dc20   91-43047
                                                          CIP

Typeset by Inforum Typesetting, Portsmouth
Printed in Great Britain by Biddles Limited, Guildford and Kings Lynn

For Duncan and Willie

Contents

List of tables and figures

List of tables

List of figures

Why the book was written

It has been my great good fortune in 30 years of professional involvement in education, to have worked with some quite outstanding children, students and colleagues. During this period, which has also involved 20 years of part-time study, I have been fortunate enough to have been involved in a wide range of research, to have had the opportunity to study research reports and to listen to the discussion of eminent researchers.

Now, from the position of sole teacher in a rural school it is my intention to attempt to provide an overview of research and development in the area of language and literacy over the past 40 years, and from it to construct a theoretically sound framework which teachers may adapt to their own needs in trying to make sense of the myriad changes with which they are being asked to cope, and in the daily decision making in which they are involved.

The experience of study and observation in which I have been involved has left me with greater enthusiasm for teaching, greater respect for my students, as well as greater pleasure in beginning to make a little more sense of the complex processes of learning and teaching.

That is what I would like to share in this book. In order to do this it is necessary to start by looking at the wider picture of what we know about children's language and learning.

Acknowledgements

The ideas and suggestions presented in this book are not new, they derive from experience, from reading and from discussion. Those who have contributed to my reading development include my parents, teachers, students and pupils. To them, too many to mention individually, I owe a tremendous debt of gratitude.

However, mention must be made of the following: Lynn Hollyer, John Monnington and Pam Rivaz, dear friends and colleagues for many years in Hertfordshire; Julie Ramsden and Tove Kettner Heiberg; Professor Margaret Clark for her kindness and willingness to listen; and Dr L. John Chapman who has given so generously of his time to discuss the ideas contained within these pages. I thank them for their trust and confidence.

I am also grateful to the many teachers and pupils who allowed me to work in their schools. Among them I am particularly grateful to Gill Simmonds in Cambridgeshire and Robin Menzies in Hertfordshire.

More recently I must acknowledge the support of the pupils, staff, parents and Board of Largue School; of my headteacher colleagues in Gordon, particularly Margaret Michie at Forgue; and of Andrew Dick, Area Education Manager for Gordon.

I am grateful to Christian Trampenau for permission to use his delightful photographs and to the proprietors of 'The Huntly Express' for permission to use two leader articles.

Finally, to my family, thank you for your tolerance, love and humour.

CHAPTER 1

Changing views of children's language and learning

The second half of the twentieth century has seen a considerable shift in attitude in the way in which linguists, psychologists, teachers and parents view children's language and learning.

Changing perspectives on language

The work of Noam Chomsky (1957, 1965) drew attention to the complex nature of language and its enormous creative potential. With this came the realization of the enormous task of language learning achieved by most children in the first few years of their lives. The studies of language development emanating from this starting point have demonstrated and emphasized language acquisition as an active rule constructing, hypothesis testing process with the emphasis firmly on the child's learning rather than on the adult's teaching (McNeill 1966, Slobin 1971, Brown 1973). The findings conflicted directly with the prevailing behaviourist psychological accounts of learning. The nature and intensity of the controversy is evident in Chomsky's 1959 review of B.F. Skinner's *Verbal Behaviour.* That Chomsky and his associates claimed language learning as a special case was partly a measure of the inadequacy of the existing psychological theories of learning to accommodate the evidence presented.

Alongside this changing view of language learning there was an increase in the size of the linguistic units studied, from individual words (Templin 1957) to grammatical relations in clauses or sentences (Brown and Bellugi 1964). The view of language learning as increasing competence in the generation of syntactically regular utterances has in turn given way to a recognition of the importance of the development of language use and its relationship to its social and cultural setting. Such development in the study of children's language was partly in response to the criticism of philosophers, sociologists and anthropologists for whom language was also a traditional area of study; but it was also a process of development from within the community of linguists. Dell Hymes (1968) introduced the concept of communicative competence, to take some account of language use and setting, while Campbell and Wales (1970) were among the first to question the syntax driven accounts of language acquisition, and Halliday's 1975 account of his son's language development was a study of the development of language functions against social contexts.

As soon as language use is considered, the focus begins to move towards language as a form of communication and towards a recognition of the importance of human interaction in the development of language.

Improvements in technology enabled Trevarthen (1974) to record on film and on videotape the genesis of human communicative interaction within the first few months of life. Evidence gathered on lightweight microphones enabled Wells (1982) in his longitudinal study of language development, to claim that communication develops when adult and child or child and child are attending to the same thing. Further technical developments along this line have enabled Tizard *et al.* (1981) to compare children's communication in the nursery school with their communication at home; and Clark *et al.* (1985) to compare children's developing discourse skills between nursery school or class and a range of school settings in the first year in school.

When due regard is given to the role of interaction in language development then the focus shifts from concern with linguistic form in isolation, to language as communication and to language organization beyond the sentence.

However, as Enkvist (1981) points out (apart from the study of texts under the heading of rhetoric) text and discourse linguistics is hardly more than ten years of age. Even within the area of text and discourse Enkvist goes on to describe a widening of interest from: 'syntactically describable cohesion through semantic coherence to patterns of human interaction' (1981: 2).

This would seem to parallel the move from reductionism already outlined in the study of language development.

Changing perspectives on learning

Similar developments have occurred in psychological views of learning, with a shift from concern with perception and simple learning tasks to interest in the relationship between perception, comprehension and other complex cognitive abilities.

Among developmental psychologists the shift has not been so drastic; there has been a continuing acceptance that a child's perspective may differ from an adult's; and there has been a focus on the nature of knowledge and the development of thought, befitting a discipline influenced over such a long period by Piaget and his genetic epistemology. Where movement among developmental psychologists does appear is in greater attention to the total context of experimental work including the experimenter's use of language, the subject's perception of the task, the apparatus used, as well as a recognition of the importance of communicative interaction between subjects and its contribution to problem tackling and solving (Donaldson 1978, Donaldson *et al.* 1983, Grieve and Hughes 1990).

Similarly, clinical psychologists attempting to assess children with language difficulties, have moved from tests of vocabulary like the English Picture Vocabulary Test (Brimer and Dunn 1962) to the assessment of discourse skills using tools such as the Preschool Language Assessment Instrument (Blank *et al.* 1978), that may be adapted to the analysis of discourse in naturalistic settings (Blank and Milewski, unpublished observations, Robson 1983).

At the time that technological advances were enabling linguists to record children's language development, other technological advances permitted the foundations of the study of artificial intelligence to be laid, and cognitive psychologists were beginning to view human beings as extremely complex information processors. This was combined with a shift from a concern with perception and simple learning to the relationship between perception, comprehension and other complex cognitive abilities.

Changing perspectives on reading

The study of reading by cognitive psychologists provides a clear example of a changing attitude to the process. Concern has moved from the visual or auditory perception of shapes, letters and sounds to the recognition of reading as a complex cognitive process involving the processing of visual language. This shift has been documented by Gibson and Levin (1975) and later by Reid (1983, 1990). Again one may perceive the move from simple processes to more complex and from small units of language to larger units. The trends can be seen to come together in the collaborative work of Kintsch, a cognitive psychologist, and van Dijk, a text linguist (1978). Indeed, the Kintsch and van Dijk paper had the highest citation rate in reading research papers for 1982 (Guthrie *et al.* 1983).

Changing educational perspectives

The insights gained from the research already referred to have caused educationists to reconsider some of their assumptions about children and learning. It is quite clear from the evidence that children are already experienced learners when they come into school; for a number of years they have been controlling their own learning as they have attempted to make sense of the world around them; and much of this learning seems to have taken the form of constructing and testing their own hypotheses. In the light of this, it is important for teachers to find out what children 'know' when they come to school. The number of studies in this area is steadily increasing (Clark 1976, Bissex 1980, Ferreiro and Teberosky 1982, Goelman *et al.* 1984, Jones 1990).

In terms of curriculum development it has focused attention on learning strategies which emphasize the child as a learner and the teacher as a resourcer (Nisbet and Shucksmith 1986).

Another shift in education attendant on the campaigns of the seventies to abolish adult illiteracy, has been the recognition of the increasingly complex literacy demands of modern technological society (Merritt 1977, Jansen 1982).

A fourth shift in education in Britain during this time has been the change from a rigidly selective state secondary school system to a less stratified one. The increasing demands that such changes have made on teachers are discussed by Lunzer and Gardner (1979) and by Chapman (1983a) with particular reference to reading development.

A fifth shift deriving from this has been the closer involvement of schools with the community. This has had two sources, one has been bottom-up where schools have developed closer links between the school, parents and the wider community, regarding parents and the school environment as a valuable and relevant resource in a continuum where schooling is not seen as discontinuous with the worlds of pre-school and post-school. At one end of this continuum there is greater involvement of parents and at the other end there is greater involvement with employers and industry. The other source has been top-down with legislation giving parents and representatives of the community greater power in school management and organization. This has been accompanied by the development of national curricula, an extension of testing and a review of examinations and profiling which bring vocational education into schools and at the same time increase the percentage of young people who are examined. The rate and extent of this change has been such that no detailed analysis of the literacy demands involved has been considered.

Summary of changing views

In summary, in the study of language, learning and education, over the past 40 years, ten trends have been identified.

- A move from the study of small units of language to the study of whole texts or sequences of discourse.
- A move in interest from the study of simple texts to the study of more complex ones.
- A move away from the study of isolated individuals to the study of interaction.
- A move from attempts to make the settings of studies of language and learning as neutral as possible to the use of naturalistic settings.
- An appreciation of the learning and ways of knowing that children bring with them to school.
- A move of concern from teaching methods to learning strategies.
- An awareness of the increasingly complex literacy demands of modern technological society.
- A move of concern from the education of an élite to education for all.
- Changing patterns of employment which mean that education may be seen as continuous and lifelong.
- Changing expectations of children, parents, community and central government.

Overall, there has been a recognition of the need to view language as communication, and an admission of the importance of the social and cultural setting of any human interaction.

Practical implications for teaching and learning then should focus upon

- The choice and structure of texts used in school – not only in terms of vocabulary and sentence structure but also the patterning of the overall text.
- The development of criteria for monitoring progression in texts used and produced – so that movement from the simple to the more complex may be structured to meet pupil needs.
- The development and extension of group and paired reading and writing – building on the learning support provided by discussion and human interaction.
- The development of comfortable, reassuring and naturalistic contexts for reading and writing – where confidence, motivation and learning may develop.

- The development of ways of finding out what children already know about and expect from written language – to capitalize on the resources of the child, the home and the wider cultural community.
- The development of appropriate learning strategies rather than a reliance on materials alone.
- The exploitation of information technology to support, extend and enhance literacy development.
- Extending and supporting the quality of literacy experience and competence of all children.
- The development of an attitude and confidence in dealing with written language that welcomes problem tackling, problem solving and change as a challenge.
- Increased confidence and competence on the part of professional educators to share their expertise with others.

Summary

In this chapter attention has been drawn to changing views of children's language and learning that have derived from research over the past 40 years. Some have derived from technological advances in the means of collecting data, some have derived from careful observation and some from collaboration across disciplines. These changes have been listed and a focus for practical implications for teaching and learning has been drawn up. Reading is viewed as communication, and as such, like any other form of human interaction the social and cultural context are of prime importance.

CHAPTER 2

Reading in this changing context

Introduction

According to Maxwell (1974) a major source of confusion in reading research is the use of the term reading without a clear statement of the sense in which it is being used. Differences in usage are probably most economically encapsulated in Gray's (1960) much-quoted description of reading as reading the lines, reading between the lines and reading beyond the lines. The term is used to describe a continuum of behaviours stretching from grapheme phoneme matching to Ronald Morris's (1976) vision of reading maturity, which seems to be rationality in the context of print.

But the concern of educators must necessarily be with reading in its widest sense, based on language but inseparable from thought. Educationists are not concerned solely with the acquisition of a discrete skill but with the development of a means to extend thought, learning and independence, as well as emotional and aesthetic experience. The strength of the wider definitions is that they permit reading to be viewed as communication between reader and writer through the text (J. Anderson 1983).

Models of the reading process

Models of the reading process differ also, reflecting varying definitions of reading and the individual and professional perspectives of the model maker.

A characteristic of changing models of the reading process in the past 40 years, as suggested in the previous chapter, is their increasing complexity. During this time reading has come to be recognized as a highly complex cognitive process involving much more than just perceptual skill. It is from insights gained from the confluence of work on perception, memory, psycholinguistics and information processing by Neisser (1967, 1976), Miller (1967, 1972, 1973), Kolers (1968, 1972, 1973), that has emerged the theoretical standpoints of writers such as Goodman (1968), Smith (1971), Clay (1972) and Gibson and Levin (1975). This influence can be seen clearly in the following statement from Gibson and Levin (1975: 11):

> Reading is not memorizing paired associates. It requires much more complex psychological processes of strategic search, organization for remembering, use of natural units in problem solving, the discovery of rules and order, and the economical use of them. Above all it requires the ability to transfer knowledge of rules and economical strategies to new material, something a child has to learn to do for himself.

The second impetus to a reassessment of the nature of the reading process came from the studies of linguistics and language acquisition of the sixties. Models such as that of Gough (1972: 354) stress the sequential processing of small units of language in the reading process:

> It has been argued (e.g. by Goodman (1970) and others) that reading is normally a kind of guessing game, in which the reader uses the printed word for little more than hints as to whether he is thinking the right thoughts or not . . . In the model I have outlined, the Reader is not a guesser. From the outside he appears to go from print to meaning as if by magic. But I have contended that this is an illusion, that he really plods through the sentence, letter by letter, word by word.

On the other hand, the reading models of Smith and of Goodman reflect concern with larger units of language, and the recognition and use of the linguistic patterning of syntactic and semantic relationships. Smith sees reading as a process by which the readers predict their way through a text, eliminating some alternatives in advance on the basis of their knowledge of the redundancy of language, and acquiring just enough visual information to eliminate the alternatives remaining. Similarly, Goodman stresses the importance of linguistic cues (semantic, syntactic and grapho/phonic) in reading and refers to it as a psycholinguistic guessing game (1970).

However, it is essential to remember that the linguistic view within which both Smith and Goodman were working was Chomskyan, sentence-based, transformational generative grammar. Valuable as such an approach has been, it is subject to the limitations outlined in the previous section with regard to studies of language development, as well as raising specific problems related to the reading process (E. Anderson 1979, and de Beaugrande, unpublished observations). A major achievement of such models, however, was to shift the emphasis of reading as a perceptual skill to viewing reading in a language context (Clark 1976). The point is put succinctly by Ferreiro and Teberosky (1982): 'Reading is not deciphering. Writing is not copying from a model.'

This stance is consonant with the view of language development as the increasing control of rule-governed or patterned behaviour, through which children attempt to make sense of the world around them.

However, as already noted, the language descriptions from which they derive, have little to say about the organization of language beyond the sentence, and fail to accommodate, except under the heading of semantics, the complex social and cultural interaction involved in communication. Indeed, in acknowledgement of this weakness Goodman (1982) has added pragmatics to his list of cue systems available to the reader in his model of the reading process.

The third group of reading models tend to combine the other two. This interactive group of reading models derives from work on comprehension carried out by those interested in cognitive psychology, artificial intelligence and text linguistics. Before dealing with these models emanating from studies of comprehension it would seem wise to consider the concept of comprehension.

If reading is an elusive concept then reading comprehension is even more so. Lunzer (1976) has described comprehension as the willingness and ability to reflect on what is read, and this provides some indication of the variability and idiosyncracy of the activity. Robinson (1977: 60–61) presents a useful summary of the variables involved:

> reading comprehension is the difference between what someone knew about a topic prior to the reading and what he or she 'winds up with' or possesses following reading. This information gain is always modulated by the individual reader. Factors which influence information gain are the nature of the learner, the nature of the material, the nature of the purposes for reading, and the means used for measurement . . . Hence, a given reader's comprehension may differ widely from week to week, day to day, moment to moment, dependent on the nature of the content and the attitudes of the writer.

Though more recent writers such as Cairney (1990) might not agree with this definition of reading comprehension as information transfer, they would see it as more of a meaning constructing activity, the listing of variables is still salutary.

Indeed, in a similar vein Chapman (1983a) gives a timely warning about over-concern with the static product comprehension, which produces no new insights of pedagogic value, to the neglect of improved understanding of the dynamic processes of comprehending. This argument would seem to bear some similarity to Vygotsky's statements with regard to the pedagogic value of finding out not what children can do on their own, but what with some instruction or teaching they can learn to do (in Donaldson *et al.* 1983).

Any concern with comprehending that is to provide insights of educational application clearly must take account of language that extends beyond the boundaries of single sentences. However, it is only in the past 15 years or so that linguists such as Halliday and Hasan (1976, 1980) in their discussion of textual cohesion and van Dijk (1977a) on the topic of discourse comprehension, have provided descriptions of language beyond the level of the sentence, and that a number of approaches to the application of discourse analysis to texts has emerged. For example, Carpenter and Just (1977a, b) in their work on cohesion and comprehension within paragraphs make use of the concept of a discourse pointer which they describe as:

> a symbol in the comprehender's mind that indicates the current topic of the discourse or the perceptual context. (1977a: 217)

> The speaker can appeal to the perceptual context to supply information for the listener's discourse pointer and thereby make assumptions about the shared contextual information. In written discourse, the writer and reader are removed in time and space, so the pointer must be controlled almost entirely through the devices of language itself. (1977a: 231)

It is worth noting at this point that Carpenter and Just's stance is text-based, emphasizing textual controls of discourse processing such as sentence structure, and the manner in which sentence structure reflects the coherent organization of discourse with respect to both the thematic organization of the topic and the propositional structure of the text. The thematic organization refers to the organization of the topic or theme of the discourse and the propositional structure refers to the underlying semantic representation of a simple sentence. Kintsch's (1977) approach, on the other hand, is schema-based, emphasizing the manner in which prior knowledge is used to reduce the set of propositions in the text. However, van Dijk (1977b) makes use of both text-based and schema-based conceptions of discourse structure, thus enabling him to discuss both bottom-up analyses starting with the text and top-down analyses of processes starting with the reader's expectations and prior knowledge. As Fredericksen (1977: 319) points out:

> An adequate account of comprehension ultimately will have to involve a detailed explication both of how text-based comprehension utilizes textual and propositional information and of the role of schema-based processes in comprehension.

Certain similarities in approach may be perceived in the third group of models of the reading process. Such models are claimed to be explicitly interactive in nature, neither strictly bottom-up as Gough (1972) nor strictly top-down as Smith (1971), so that information is considered to be processed simultaneously from several knowledge sources (Rumelhart 1977). Stanovich (1980, 1986) goes further and proposes an interactive model of reading combined with an assumption of compensatory processing:

> that a deficit in any particular process will result in a greater reliance on other knowledge sources, regardless of their level in the processing hierarchy. (1980: 32)

This he claims provides the most adequate account for the pattern of results in the research literature.

Models of the reading process proliferate and as Venezky (1976: 44) wryly observes:

> From all these uncertainties, there is some comfort to be derived for our humanistic souls from the observation that the average child has considerably less trouble in learning to read than psychologists and linguists do in defining reading.

Interactive models of the reading process

Perhaps what we should be looking for is a wider view of communication and human interaction within which to set models of the reading process. There would appear to be two approaches which attempt to do so. One is de Beaugrande's (1981) attempt to produce a science of texts from a synthesis of 'traditional beyond-the-sentence linguistics with a wide range of interdisciplinary research on the production, reception and utilization of texts in human interaction'. The strength of de Beaugrande's work is the breadth of vision it embraces, building on a textlinguistic base but also accommodating work from the whole range of cognitive sciences. This is made explicit in his statement that the intensity of reading research possibly signals that it may be a test case for 'a new outlook on a science of cognition and communication' (de Beaugrande, unpublished observations: 49).

The other approach stresses the social rather than the cognitive aspects of human interaction, and is based on the work of Halliday and his view of language as a social semiotic. Halliday (1974) contrasts the 'language as knowledge' or intra-organism approach of linguists such as Chomsky and psychologists such as Miller with Halliday's own approach to language as inter-organism. This is in the British linguistic tradition, deriving particularly from the work of Malinowski and of Firth, with its emphasis on the relevance for meaning of the 'context of situation'. Basic to any understanding of Halliday's work then are the concepts of 'language as a social semiotic' and 'context of situation'. It is misleading to consider any aspect of Halliday's work without an understanding of these central concepts. He uses 'language as a social semiotic' to describe his perspective in which he regards language as:

> simply one among a number of systems of meaning that are the property that constitutes human culture

and attempts

> to relate language to one particular area, one particular higher order semiotic, namely that of social structure. (Halliday and Hasan 1980: 5)

The term 'context of situation' was coined by Malinowski (1923) in his anthropological studies. In Halliday's use of the term, related to the study of language, it is the context in which the text occurs. Halliday uses a fairly simple conceptual framework to describe the context of situation:

1. The field of discourse refers to what is happening, to the nature of the social action that is taking place.
2. The tenor of discourse refers to who is taking part, to the nature of the participants, their statuses, roles and relationships.
3. The mode of discourse refers to the part language is playing, what it is that the participants are expecting the language to do for them in that situation: the symbolic organization of the text, the status that it has, and its function in the context, including the channel, whether spoken or written, and the rhetorical mode, what is being achieved by the text in terms of such categories as persuasive, expository, didactic.

However, as Halliday points out (Halliday and Hasan 1980), as well as 'context of situation', Malinowski considered the 'context of culture' an essential requirement for adequate understanding of a text. Halliday presents the relationship between the 'context of culture' and the 'context of situation' in the form reproduced in Figure 1.

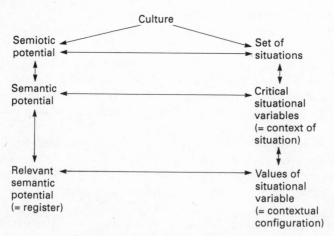

Figure 1   The relationship between the context of culture and the context of situation (Halliday and Hasan 1980: 19)

This approach then would seem to provide a strong socio-cultural background to what have been to date, predominantly psychological and linguistic models of the reading process. It is only recently that attempts have been made to construct models of the reading process within a systemic–functional or Hallidayan view of language (Gerot 1983). As Enkvist (1981: 1) points out, of all approaches to linguistics, Halliday's appears most apt for extension into the areas of cognition and interaction because:

> It has always emphasized the importance of textual, interpersonal and func-
> tional aspects of language. By so doing, it has discussed problems of interac-
> tion that have been ignored by, or wilfully excluded from many other linguistic
> theories of the past half century.

The linguistic aspect of Halliday's work that has received some atten-
tion in reading research has been the notion of cohesion. Unfortunately, in studies of reading development, this has often been abstracted from the Hallidayan overview of language, and consequently its power as a research tool has been weakened. Mosenthal and Tierney (1984) review some of the pitfalls attendant on such practice, though they fail to identify the underlying cause.

A new model of the reading process

It will be argued now, as does Chapman (1987), that a model of reading within a systemic functional description of language as a social semiotic, particularly with the inclusion of the notion of cohesion, provides a useful tool for teachers concerned with reading development.

The nub of any model of reading must be the relationship between the reader, the writer and the text. A physical analogy of two people on a see-saw may be useful in clarifying the relationship. The aim is to bring the see-saw or text into a state of balance between the writer and the reader. Since it is an analogy with written communication then neither participant can see, hear or speak to the other. They can only communicate through the see-saw or text. The more they know about each other in terms of likely height, weight, personality and intention, the more efficiently will they complete their task. Neither the writer nor the reader alone can accom-
plish the task; each must take account of the other and communicate through the text.

What is being presented is a tricorne approach, which can overcome the weaknesses of Mosenthal and Tierney's position between the two horns of their dilemma, between the reader and the text. It goes beyond the simplis-
tic readability notions of matching reader to text, to the more complex task

of matching readers and all their social and cultural expectations and assumptions about the texts in question and their writers, to the writers and all their social and cultural expectations and assumptions about the texts and their readers.

The overriding strength of this model is that it permits this reciprocity between writer and reader within the interpersonal function of language, while not neglecting the ideational or textual function of written discourse.

This is in direct contrast with the schema-based models of comprehension that emphasize the ideational function of texts to the exclusion of both the interpersonal and the textual functions, to the extent that some of the arguments followed through to their logical conclusion suggest that we can only read what we already know and that we cannot learn anything new from reading written texts.

If this is the case, then one must wonder why so much time is spent on teaching children to read. Clearly, it is not the case. One of the undisputed and most important aspects of literature is its power to extend experience and empathy to groups, settings and situations that have not been experienced at first hand. Similar extension of experience and understanding may be achieved through non-fiction texts. To argue otherwise is to argue against the very notions of independent learning and distance teaching through the use of the written word. The success of the Open University alone would seem to be evidence against this. Despite its original name of the University of the Air, the most effective elements of the courses are the written texts.

This model is consonant with the major points already presented in the earlier chapter of this book. It takes account of reading as both a linguistic and a cognitive process. It permits the social and cultural setting of reader, text and writer to be considered. It is clearly concerned with language at the discourse level, as language in use and as communication. It is of a form that is easily translated into classroom terms while retaining sufficient linguistic detail to permit it to be used to diagnose strengths and weaknesses in writers, texts and readers. It is also close to the model applied successfully by Steffensen (1981) in her research on reading comprehension across cultures; as stringent a test as any.

Summary

Three broad types of reading model were introduced: (1) bottom-up, starting with the smallest units of language; (2) top-down, starting with larger units of meaning; and (3) interactive models, which involve the flexible use of all cue systems. It was suggested that an interactive compensatory model of reading set within a Hallidayan view of language as communication and an aspect of human interaction would prove a useful tool for teachers concerned with reading development. This model takes account of the reader, the writer and the text, concerned as it is with interpersonal interaction, content and text features.

CHAPTER 3

Applying a new model to classroom practice

The limited impact of earlier models on practice

There have been few attempts to produce models of reading directly applicable to the practice of reading development in the classroom. Even work on phoneme grapheme correspondence has been slow to percolate to the classroom (Morris 1979, Southgate *et al.* 1981). In the late 1940s and 1950s the major debate concerned whether phonics or look and say should be the approach to initial literacy. These approaches reflected the views of learning and of the nature of reading of the day. They were to be seen most clearly in the resources used rather than necessarily in the practice, which in most cases continued to be fairly eclectic (DES 1975).

The impact of the developments in linguistics and psychology, outlined in the first chapter, indicated the limitations of such approaches and raised serious questions of the nature of reading development beyond the initial stages of instruction. The model of reading presented in the Bullock Report (DES 1975) simply described reading development as consisting of the acquisition of primary skills, intermediate skills and comprehension skills. It is representative of the period of transition in which it was produced, owing some allegiance, if only in name, to behaviourist skills training approaches to learning, while overall it does not look unlike a Smith or Goodman model of reading, with regard to the use of syntactic cues in the section on intermediate skills, while the comprehension skills section fully recognizes the literacy demands of modern technological society.

However, the extent to which schools were developing reading beyond the initial stages was limited, as revealed in the two Schools Council projects in the area – *Extending Beginning Reading* (Southgate *et al.* 1981) and *The Effective Use of Reading* (Lunzer and Gardner 1979).

Professional interest in the notion of cohesion

Some recognition of teacher education needs in this respect had been made with the Open University course 'Reading Development' and later the Reading Diploma and MA courses. It was from the 'Reading Development' and 'Language Development' courses and the continuing requests from teachers for guidance in this area that developed Chapman's (1983b) interest in the usefulness of the notion of cohesion in reading development education and his research on the development of children's perception of textual cohesion in school texts (1984, 1987).

In summary, Halliday's view of language would seem to accommodate some of the increased expectations both of model makers of the reading process and of teachers and pupils.

Reading is now perceived as being a complex communicative process. Any model of reading must take account then of the processing of complete texts, and of the social and cultural context in which reader and writer interact. Interactive compensatory models of the reading process would seem to be more powerful if placed within a wider social view of language in use, such as that of Halliday (1974, 1985) and Halliday and Hasan (1976, 1980).

The literacy demands on adults are also complex. It is no longer enough to be able to read the words on the page; a truly literate person must bear the source of the text, the writer, in mind and actively interrogate the text, as the Bullock Report (DES 1975) puts it. It may be necessary to know about the background of writers, why they choose to write on a particular subject, why they ask those particular questions, or why they choose to express themselves in one way or in another. Such questioning may enhance understanding of a text and assist in the perception of gaps in arguments and in the detection of occasions when the discourse is being manipulated to support a weak or tenuous case (Coulon 1983).

However, from the existing observational studies of reading in classrooms (Lunzer and Gardner 1979, Southgate *et al.* 1981, Nicholson 1983) such close questioning of texts appears to be the exception rather than the rule in schools.

In pedagogical terms, and in terms of the developments outlined in the first section of this volume, the crucial learning situation would seem to be the one where child and adult share a text, and in that sharing, begin to see the writers behind the texts and to question the writers' linguistic choices and their thinking. Alongside this will develop awareness of the organization of discourse and the options open to the writer.

Chapman (1983a), writing on the subject of reading development, presents as valuable insights for practising teachers, some knowledge of text linguistics and, in particular, proposes Halliday's systemic functional grammar as being more appropriate to teaching than most others. In addition, he recommends, as of particular usefulness to teachers, factors which so often remain implicit:

> Amongst such factors are language variety, including the language of books, the register of instruction, the theme of a story and different types of text and cohesion. (1983a: 47)

Chapman goes on to claim that communication through texts relies on linguistic knowledge or awareness as well as prior or world knowledge.

If, as Halliday and Hasan (1980) suggest, chains of cohesive ties are mechanisms for keeping track of people, objects and places in texts; for joining parts of texts together; and for defining the content domain of text; then children's developing awareness of these chains, and teachers' awareness of their function, would indeed seem to be of central importance in the development of reading. An explanation and summary of these ties as presented in Appendix 1.

The place of comprehension in the model

Linda Gerot (1983) has addressed this issue in her paper 'Reading comprehension and the systemic–functional model of language'. In it she discusses the relationship between context, function and form and stresses that because of this systemic relationship one is able to infer from situation to text, and from text to situation. Her model of comprehension is from the perspective of the role of language in context:

> Comprehension comes about when the reader responds to the meanings mapped onto the linguistic elements, both structural and non-structural and when he responds to the context of situation which is reconstituted through the language patterns of the text. In understanding a text, the reader takes into account all he knows about what is going on, what part the language is playing and what participants are involved. (1983: 12)

This brings together the points made by Halliday and Hasan (1980) that the field of discourse, since it determines to a large part the content, influences selection from the transitivity systems of grammar; the tenor of discourse, related to the participants and their social relation, influences the selection of mood and modality; while the mode of discourse, concerned as it is with the channel and register, influences the texture, the internal organization of each clause in terms of theme, and information organization as well as the cohesive relations between clauses and sentences.

Studies of cohesion and reading

These studies were reviewed by Chapman (1987) in a companion volume. One important point that emerges is that the early research of the 1960s and 1970s (Chai 1967, Bormuth *et al.* 1970, Lesgold 1974, Richek 1976/77) was concerned mainly with the perception of personal pronouns, and the texts used tended to be pairs of sentences or brief passages. Writing in 1980, Moberly was able to claim that:

> No empirical study found has considered the four types of anaphora as identified by Halliday and Hasan; nor has the location of the anaphoric form and its presupposition (immediate, mediated, or remote) been a factor in any empirical study. (1980: 21)

She attempted to rectify this situation and to resolve the conflicting findings of Bormuth *et al.* (1970) and Lesgold (1974) in her thesis of 1980. She did so by testing the differences between the understanding of four types of anaphoric relationships, in three different locations in connected discourse, by fourth- and sixth-grade subjects (nine and eleven year olds) of average or better reading ability, i.e. the subjects were given stories in which lexical, reference, substitution, and ellipsis items were placed in immediate, mediated or remote positions throughout the passages. It is interesting to note at this point that Moberly makes use of only four out of Halliday and Hasan's (1976) five cohesive categories. She makes no mention of the category of conjunction. Sixty subjects, 30 in each age group, were randomly selected from a population of average or above average readers, as measured by the SRA Reading Comprehension Test. They were required to identify and write down the presupposed items of the underlined anaphoric forms. Significant differences were found between the age groups, among anaphoric types and between tie locations.

However, her findings did not resolve the contradictory results of Bormuth *et al.* (1970) and Lesgold (1974). Bormuth *et al.* subjects found personal pronouns to be among the most difficult of the different anaphoric items tested, whereas Lesgold subjects found them relatively easy. Though it must be noted at this point that Lesgold used different measures of comprehension. Bormuth *et al.* tested fourth-grade children. The study looked at simple anaphora, which had an antecedent contained in the sentence immediately preceding the one containing the anaphoric form. These sentences were then embedded in a four- or five-sentence paragraph, which was below, or at, fourth-grade level of difficulty, according to the Dale–Chall readability formula. The results demonstrated that many of the students had a very poor understanding of the syntactical structures which were under examination. Lesgold considered that the Bormuth study had been weakened by the fact that, on occasion, the correct answer was the only one that was semantically possible. Lesgold also dismissed the hierarchical ranking of anaphoric forms which had been suggested by Bormuth *et al.*, because there had been no control procedures to ensure that the ranking was established only on the syntactical difficulty, and was not due to other factors. Even at this stage the fact that cohesive devices have a syntactic and semantic role was causing difficulty for empirical researchers. Lesgold's (1974) study used nine of Bormuth's anaphoric forms with third- and fourth-grade children. He reported a different hierarchy of understanding of the anaphoric forms and concluded that the fourth-grade children were capable of understanding most forms in some contexts.

In fact Moberly's results support the hierarchies of neither Bormuth *et al.* nor Lesgold. She does point out that this could be due to the fact that both Bormuth *et al.* and Lesgold tested anaphoric relationships in the immediate location only. In addition, her format of testing also differed from both. What is of particular interest in Moberly's work is her conclusion drawn from the two significant interactions of anaphoric form × tie location, and age × anaphoric form × tie location, that the variables of anaphoric type and tie location cannot be considered separately.

Further evidence on this matter was provided by Nunan (1983 a, b) in a study of secondary age children's ability to relate the two parts of a cohesive tie within secondary school texts. The subjects in this study found it significantly easier to replace deletions whose antecedent existed within the same sentence than those requiring the integration of information across the sentence boundary even when the items deleted were identical in type.

This question of tie location, in a slightly different form, was taken up by Hadley (1985) in an empirical investigation concerned with the relationship between the understanding of cohesive items and comprehension, and the perception of anaphoric items placed within quoted speech. The subjects were 151 primary schoolchildren from three year levels. Twelve anaphoric personal pronouns were embedded in passages of continuous text. The results showed a significant relationship between the understanding of the selected anaphoric personal reference items and general ability in reading, as measured by a standardized test. Children at all levels found the items set within direct speech, more difficult to comprehend than the items in the rest of the text. A more recent study by Lewis and Harrison (1988) confirms this finding when a referent location test was used with primary schoolchildren. The subjects found it significantly easier to locate the referents of six pronouns in indirect speech then in direct speech. Interestingly, such differences did not occur when a cloze task was employed.

It would appear that despite some contradictions in findings there is an increasing body of evidence that suggests that many children experience difficulty in resolving cohesive ties in some texts and in some contexts. The results suggest that tie distance and location in direct speech may be significant. Although most studies have been concerned with the resolution of pronouns, Gardner's work on logical connectives in science texts (1977, 1983) indicates clearly the difficulties experienced by average secondary-school students with connectives drawn from their science texts.

The largest scale study of cohesion and reading was carried out by Chapman at the Open University and is reported by him in the first book in this series (Chapman 1987). This consisted of a study of 1,355 children aged eight years, ten years and 13 years on three occasions at yearly intervals, so that on the final occasion the pupils were aged ten years, 12 years and 15 years. Drawing on the existing research on cloze studies (J. Anderson 1976, Harrison 1980 and Chapman 1983a) Chapman made use of a modified form of cloze procedure to assess the subjects' perception of textual cohesion. The reasoning was as follows. Reading in school/learning situations is predominantly silent. This being the case, some adjustment or intervention in the reading process is necessary to make it accessible to the researcher. The commonest approach to this task is to set comprehension questions on the passages read. As Tuinman (1973/74) demonstrated, some children can answer questions without reading the passage. That is, questions may vary in their passage dependency. In many cases it is difficult to construct questions that are not themselves more difficult to read than the passages. This approach was discarded for these reasons.

At the time of developing the methodology Chapman was impressed by the richness of the data provided by Goodman's oral miscue analysis and the quality of insight which this provided for the teacher interacting with individual children. However, what was required according to Chapman was:

> a method that allowed many texts of some length to be read silently by many children in normal classroom conditions yet retaining the ability to detect textlinguistic growth. (1987: 58)

The solution was to delete one end of a cohesive tie in a text and to invite the subject to replace the word that they thought the writer would have used. The cohesive ties chosen were from a prominent chain of ties running through the text. The result is a modified form of text which has the considerable advantage that the items for deletion are not randomly chosen, but are items from the chains which Halliday and Hasan (1980) claim are devices by which we keep track of people, objects and places in texts, by which parts of text are joined together and by which the content domain of the text is defined. The powerfulness of this tool is reinforced when we consider Oller's (1979: 347) statement about the distinguishing quality of the much blunter instrument the traditional nth word deletion cloze text:

they require the utilization of discourse level costraints as well as structural constraints within sentences. Probably it is this distinguishing characteristic which makes cloze tests so robust and which generates their surprisingly strong validity coefficients in relation to other pragmatic procedures.

The problem remains of summating data over different passages. However, this was addressed in two ways. In the first place the comparison was of the same children's responses to the same passages on three occasions, so that the passages and deletions were kept constant. Secondly, a number of common passages were used across the three age ranges so that responses to these might be analysed across age ranges and occasion of testing.

It was considered that with increasing age and experience of using texts, ability to perceive cohesive ties and chains, as measured by the ability to replace deleted items from ties and chains, would also increase.

In the youngest group and the middle group all children in the appropriate age group, in attendance at the schools during the testing sessions, were included in the sample. In the oldest age group English sets were sampled to provide a full range of ability. In addition, any subjects expressing excessive anxiety about the task, or failing to complete at least two-thirds of the test items were excluded, except for one or two young children who went through all the passages and completed what they could of the tests, i.e. fewer than two-thirds of the items were attempted. As a result of pilot tests it was decided to place the fiction and non-fiction texts in separate booklets and to provide practice booklets, to introduce the task and to give practice in doing a cloze type of exercise. Materials from local schools and libraries were surveyed and collected, and national and local surveys of children's reading interests were consulted. For example, Books one and three contained passages from reading schemes, from 'quality' children's books which are frequently read to children, as well as books which are read by children; whereas Books two and four contained passages from worksheets, textbooks and reference books. To keep as close as possible to the original texts the pages were photographed and lines of text were then adjusted to produce deletions of a standard length. The only other change made to the texts was the loss of colour in the black-and-white reproduction. In order to draw attention to the deletions a double line was inserted in each space and a number placed in the margin.

The subjects responses were punched into a computer and analysed at the first stage using the NEWGAP program developed by J. Anderson (1982a, b). This program produces a reordering of responses to each deletion according to frequency of occurrence. The number of matches with the original deleted word or words is computed and expressed as the number of matches, the proportion of matches and the proportion of mismatches. The consensus or extent to which responses cluster is presented as a coefficient, so that a consensus of 1 would mean that all subjects had produced the same response, regardless of whether it was the author's word or not; and a coefficient of 0 would mean that each subject had produced a different response. For example, from the 1980 data from the 13 year olds, from the rural schools the 168 subjects responded in the following manner to item 1 from Booklet 3:

Deleted word   MILKING

Responses	*Number*
MILKING	116
WORK	24
JOB	12
COW	4
TASK	3
DIANE	1
BURGOMASTER	1
COWSHED	1
PLAN	1
DEED	1
XXX	1
CHORE	1
SIXTEENTH	1
MILK	1
consensus	0.7741
estimated entropy	0.2259
no. different responses	14
no. of matches	116
proportion of matches	0.6905
proportion of mismatches	0.3095

In this example then, the most frequent response was milking produced by 116 subjects, the least frequent responses produced by one subject each were Diane, Burgomaster, cowshed, plan, deed, chore, sixteenth and milk. Only one subject made no response, coded as XXX. There were only 14 different responses and there was a high level of consensus 0.7741, as 152 of the 168 subjects produced one or other of the three most frequent responses. The estimated entropy measure indicates the spread of responses and is the converse of consensus. A hundred and sixteen subjects chose the author's word, the word originally deleted, and this is indicated as number of matches. The proportion of matches was 0.6905 and conversely the proportion of mismatches was 0.3095.

Useful as this information is as a rough indication of performance it is limited by its dependence on the replacement of the author's word as an index of success. No account is taken in this final section of the program of the appropriateness of responses other than those that match the author's word.

In order to deal with this a second-stage analysis was developed. The theoretical base of the approach is that of error analysis as outlined by Pit Corder (1974) and Richards (1974), and miscue analysis as presented by Goodman (1969). It is unique, however, in as much as it is applied to the analysis of responses to deleted items from cohesive chains.

The results reported by Chapman were as predicted with improvement in scores over time and with age.

Since the passages and booklets for the younger group differed from those of the other two groups direct comparisons cannot be made. However, there were five passages containing 22 deletions which were common to all the age groups over the three years. The data from these items, from the rural schools, was subjected to a second-stage analysis. The justification for allocation to groups appears in Chapman (1987: 76–88 and Appendix 5). The responses were allocated to five groups, In groups 1 and 2 there was no evidence of the perception of cohesion, while group 3 was a transition stage and groups 4 and 5 provided clear evidence of the perception of cohesion, including the author's word and synonyms in group 5. These five groups correspond to Points in Chapman's Reading Development Continuum in the following manner: group 1 = P1, group 2 = P2, group 3 = P2 transition, group 4 = P3, and group 5 = P4. The pattern of responses, analysed in such fashion, for each age group are presented as percentages in Tables 1–3.

The results are precisely as predicted with the balance of responses moving from omissions and random responses to those maintaining syntactic and semantic acceptability within the sentence, the cohesive chain from which the item was deleted and the passage as a whole.

Table 1   Second-stage analysis of the responses of the youngest age group on the 'common' items, for the three years (22 items)

	Group 1	*Group 2*	*Group 3*	*Group 4*	*Group 5*
	No evidence of perception of cohesion		*Transition*	*Evidence of preception of cohesion*	
Year					*Author's word or synonym*
1980	29.5	22.1	10	20.9	17.5
1981	22.0	19.3	11.7	25	22
1982	21.8	17.8	10.5	27.2	22.7

Table 2 Second-stage analysis of the responses of the middle age group on the 'common' items, for the three years (22 items)

	Group 1	Group 2	Group 3	Group 4	Group 5
	No evidence of perception of cohesion		*Transition*	*Evidence of preception of cohesion*	
Year					*Author's word or synonym*
1980	12.2	15.5	14.3	29.9	28.1
1981	9.2	14.1	13	30.6	33.1
1982	9.3	11.3	11	31.7	36.7

A similar pattern emerges within this age group and when viewed as an extension of the pattern displayed in the results of the younger group it can be seen that there is an increase in both groups which involve an awareness of cohesion.

In this group a similar pattern emerges, though the main move with age is from group 4 to group 5, i.e. towards the author's choice of word or a very near synonym.

Table 3 Second-stage analysis of the responses of the oldest age group on the 'common' items, for the three years (22 items)

	Group 1	Group 2	Group 3	Group 4	Group 5
	No evidence of perception of cohesion		*Transition*	*Evidence of preception of cohesion*	
Year					*Author's word or synonym*
1980	7.3	11.7	13.3	34	33.7
1981	7.5	9.3	11.5	33.3	38.4
1982	6.2	7.2	11.1	32.3	43.2

It would appear from these results that with increasing age and experience of using texts, ability to perceive cohesive ties and chains, as measured by the ability to replace deleted items from ties and chains, also increases.

The relationship between cohesion and comprehension

One possible weakness of the gap technique employed by Chapman in his longitudinal study is that it is removed from the activity of reading, in as much as the subjects are presented with mutilated text, in which words have been deleted. Consequently, one might enquire whether subjects providing acceptable responses in the gaps can fully understand the original unmutilated version of the text.

Research on the validity of cloze tests as measures of reading comprehension reviewed by J. Anderson (1976: 39) would suggest that this is the case. These studies of the correlation of cloze tests with comprehension tests based on the same passages, produced correlations ranging from 0.70 to 0.946. In all cases these were traditional nth word deletion cloze tests. Nevertheless, it was suggested that similar results would be obtained using the gap/cohesion tests. That is that there would be a high positive correlation between performance on the gap/cohesion tests and performance on comprehension tests on undeleted versions of a sample of texts from the Chapman test booklets.

A repeated measures design was employed. After the third administration of the Chapman gap/cohesion tests a comprehension test based on a sample of unmutilated texts was administered to the same pupils. This section focuses on the 15 year olds from two Cambridgeshire secondary schools.

The comprehension test was based on eight passages from the gap/cohesion test booklets (Chapman 1987); four passages from Fiction Booklet 3 and four passages from Fact Booklet 4. One hundred and sixteen questions were posed on the passages. Of these, forty-two drew on information from ties, one end of which had been deleted in the original gap/cohesion passages. For example, in the following passage from Laura Ingalls Wilder's *Little House in the Big Woods*, the reference item 'the' signalling that 'the dark syrup' in the second sentence is the 'syrup' already referred to in the first sentence, was deleted in the Chapman gap/cohesion booklet:

> One morning she boiled molasses and sugar together until they made a thick syrup, and Pa brought in two pans of clean, white snow from outdoors. Laura and Mary each had a pan, and Pa and Ma showed them how to pour the dark syrup in little streams on to the snow.

The comprehension question based on that item was:

> What was the dark syrup made of?

In order to answer this question correctly it is necessary to use information from the other end of the tie, in the first sentence. Twenty-six questions drew on information from ties not deleted in the original gap/cohesion passages. For example, the passage, already mentioned, continues:

> They made circles, and curlicues, and squiggledy things, and these hardened at once and were candy. Laura and Mary might eat one piece each, but the rest was saved for Christmas Day.

All this was done because Aunt Eliza and Uncle Peter and the cousins, Peter and Alice and Ella, were coming to spend Christmas.

The day before Christmas they came. Laura and Mary heard the gay ringing of sleigh bells, growing louder every moment, and then the big bobsled came out of the woods and drove up to the gate. Aunt Eliza and Uncle Peter and the cousins were in it, all covered up, under blankets and robes and buffalo skins.

They were wrapped up in so many coats and mufflers and veils and shawls that they looked like big, shapeless bundles.

The tie that was not deleted in the test booklet was that between 'They' in the last sentence and the characters mentioned in the previous sentence. And the question based on that tie was:

Who were wrapped up in coats and mufflers?

A question that cannot be answered correctly without reference to the previous sentence.

Sixteen questions tapped information from implicit cohesion e.g. where order implied a connective relationship. For example, in a passage from a history textbook (Bailey and Wise 1971) the following two sentences appear:

Sir Edmund's second son, Edmund, nicknamed 'Sir Mun', joined the King's forces. His eldest brother Ralph sided with Parliament.

The question on the implicit adversative or 'contrary to expectation' tie was:

Choose one of the four words to complete the sentence:
Sir Edmund's second son, Edmund, nicknamed 'Sir Mun', joined the King's forces (and)
    (but)
    (so)
    (then)
his eldest brother Ralph sided with Parliament.

A further 16 were general overall comprehension questions such as asking the pupil to produce a title for the passage. The final 16 questions were designed to tap previous knowledge of the story, the author or subject matter. For example, one such question on the history passage already mentioned was:

Who was the leader of the Parliamentary forces during the Civil War?

This was not mentioned in the passage but ability to answer the question would indicate some previous knowledge of the subject.

The deleted items tapped were examples of all sub-categories of co-hesive devices deleted in the gap/cohesion test booklets. The undeleted items tapped represented all the sub-categories deleted in the gap/

Table 4 Correlations between comprehension scores. Gap booklet scores and reading test scores for 29 subjects aged 15–16 years

	Reading scores	Gap	Comp. cats 1–4	Comp. deleted items	Comp. not deleted	Comp. implicit	General quest.	Previous know.	Fiction score	Fact score	Fiction cats. 1–4	Fact cats. 1–4	Total comp. score
Reading scores		0.59**	0.70**	0.58**	0.59**	0.45*	0.32NS	0.32NS	0.58**	0.61**	0.64**	0.55**	0.69**
Gap			0.60**	0.68**	0.36*	0.56**	0.43*	0.19NS	0.60**	0.35NS	0.64**	0.34NS	0.57**
Comp. cats 1–4				0.94**	0.88**	0.87**	0.78**	0.54**	0.89**	0.80**	0.90**	0.80**	0.99**
Comp. deleted items					0.75**	0.78**	0.64**	0.48**	0.83**	0.76**	0.84**	0.75**	0.93**
Comp. not deleted						0.68*	0.54**	0.51**	0.78**	0.74**	0.78**	0.72**	0.89**
Comp. implicit							0.69**	0.59**	0.82**	0.69**	0.80**	0.67**	0.88**
General quest.								0.31NS	0.70**	0.59**	0.68**	0.64**	0.75**
Previous know.													
Fiction score								0.54**		0.61**	0.44**	0.49**	0.65**

Fact score	0.50**	0.99**	0.48**	0.90**
Fiction cats. 1–4		0.48**	0.98**	0.83**
Fact cats. 1–4			0.45*	0.88**
Total comp. score				0.80**

Where Reading scores refers to the Reading Test Scores.
Gap refers to the Gap Booklet Scores.
Comp. cats. 1–4 refers to the Comprehension score for categories 1 to 4 (cohesive items – not previous knowledge).
Comp. deleted items refers to the Comprehension Score on those items deleted in the Gap Test Booklets.
Comp. non deleted refers to the Comprehension Score on cohesive items not deleted in the Gap Test Booklets.
Comp. implicit refers to the Comprehension Score on implicitly cohesive items, usually connection implied by sentence order.
General questions refers to the score on general comprehension questions.
Previous knowledge refers to the score on previous knowledge questions.
Fiction score refers to the score on fiction passages.
Fact score refers to the score on fact passages.
Fiction cats. 1–4 refers to the score on fiction items 1–4.
Fact cats. 1–4 refers to the score on fact items 1–4.
Total comp. score refers to the total Comprehension Score.

cohesion test booklets except for the sub-categories of substitution, but one question tapping ellipsis was included. A full analysis of the questions is presented in Appendix 2. The test was administered at the end of the third Chapman gap/cohesion data collection, under similar conditions to the other tests, but being at the end of the session there was not a high completion rate. Because of this low completion rate the results of only the group of twenty-nine subjects who omitted between zero and ten questions were analysed. The responses were scored and the results analysed using Datastat (Wood 1986) a statistics/data analysis package for BBC Microcomputers. The correlations of the subsections of the test with each other and with the Reading and Booklet scores are presented in Table 4.

There is a high correlation between all of the measures. Those with a particularly high correlation are items deleted in the Gap Booklets X Score on Comprehension items 1–4, i.e. those items other than previous knowledge; items deleted in the Gap Booklets X total comprehension score. This result would suggest that the deleted items were representative of other cohesive items and of implicit cohesive devices. The lowest correlations are all associated with the previous knowledge items. Previous knowledge of the narrative or of the subject matter did not appear to facilitate processing the texts.

In fact, the only non-statistically significant correlations are:

1. Reading test score × Previous knowledge questions.
2. Gap booklet score × Previous knowledge questions.
3. Gap booklet score × score on fact passages.
4. Gap booklet score × fact items 1–4.
5. General comprehension questions × Previous knowledge questions.

However, as predicted there was a significant correlation between the Gap Booklet Scores and the Comprehension Scores.

It is clear that the comprehension test was too long and the sample obtained is consequently rather small. Because of the length, passages were not randomized and this may account for the poorer performance on the fact passages that came in the second part of the test. However, as they stand the results are of considerable interest. Firstly, there was a high correlation between performance on the two types of test, the Gap test and the open-ended comprehension test. Despite the weakness of each there was a considerable area of agreement. Secondly, schema theorists (Anderson *et al.* 1977, Rumelhart and Ortony 1977) would have predicted a more powerful effect for previous knowledge, believing as they do that previous knowledge reduces the amount of inferencing required in reading, so that a high level of previous knowledge should facilitate comprehension as well as ease and speed of reading. However, when Johnston and Pearson (1982) examined the effects of prior knowledge, the connectedness of ideas in the text, the types of question probes and processing indices used to assess comprehension as well as reading ability and reading speed they found that, important though previous knowledge is, so also is ability. A particularly interesting finding was that the manipulation of connectivity in the passage affected only the more able readers. A possible explanation they present is that less able readers read and digest text in word or proposition units and spend little effort in integrating the units. Johnston and Pearson's study was limited to one text, but their suggestion of development in readers' use of connectivity cues is supported by the findings of the study reported here. It may be that the 29 subjects in this study were able readers to whom level of previous knowledge made little difference.

Incorporating the model into a teaching programme

If, as Moe (1978), Chapman (1983a) and Moe and Irwin (1986) have suggested, awareness of the cohesive patterning of texts contributes to reading fluency, then specific teaching to increase awareness of cohesive devices in texts should contribute to improved reading ability.

In the USA, the work of Gordon (1980) and of Hansen (1981) indicated that the ability to infer connections can be enhanced through instruction. Pulver (1983, 1986) described activities that proved effective in helping students understand connectives. Her structured approach drew on social science texts in use with 11 year olds. It progresses from work on explicit connectives in sentences to implicit connectives in continuous natural texts.

Baumann and Stevenson (1986) and Baumann (1986/87) recommend a four-stage strategy for teaching the comprehension of anaphoric relations of personal reference and substitution. Using this approach Baumann (1986/87) reports that a group of nine year olds performed better than a control group and a group using a reading scheme.

In England, Winchester (1984) claims that this occurred in her case-study, working on non-fiction texts, within a topic on the industrial revolution, with a class of ten-year-old children in a Birmingham school. Although Winchester provides examples of the teaching strategies used and two pieces of children's writing, no further data are presented.

Similar claims have been made by Wishart (1987) with regard to work with children for whom English is a second language. After six, weekly one hour sessions, led by teachers following an in-service course on the preparation of materials and approaches to help their pupils to attend to the cohesive elements of texts, alongside the conceptual content, a significant gain (at the one per cent level) was reported on a cloze passage post-test compared with the score on the same passage in the pre-test.

It was predicted in the following study that subjects who have received instruction in the functioning of cohesive ties in their own writing and in the writing of others, would have higher scores on a standardized reading test than a group which had not.

A small group study

In this study approaches were developed with a small group of 10–11-year-old children to increase their awareness of cohesive devices in texts. The approach was to incorporate awareness of cohesive devices within group reading and discussion activities of the type recommended by Lunzer and Gardner (1979), as this appeared to be the most effective strategy available for extending children's reading and provided an opportunity, through the children's justifications of their choices, to obtain some information about how they understand the text content and structure. It was also argued by Chapman and Anderson (1982) and by E. Anderson (1983a, b, 1984a) that a teacher's knowledge of cohesive patterning may improve the quality of teacher intervention in such activities. Group reading activities using cloze procedure can be enhanced if the items deleted are from a cohesive chain, thus encouraging the use of information from beyond the sentence in justifying one's choice of word. Similarly, in group sequencing activities an awareness of the patterning of the texts should assist the teacher in identifying the types of cues that are, or are not being used by the children. In group prediction the usefulness of the notion of cohesion is not quite so obvious. However, if one considers the cohesive ties to be as Halliday and Hasan (1980) suggest, mechanisms for keeping track of people, objects and places in text, for joining pieces of text together and for defining the content domain of text, then pupils' predictions of what follows in a text may be based, at least partly, on their interpretations of the mechanisms used by the writer. Perhaps the most useful, as well as interesting information for the teacher, from this source, may be how individual awareness of the content domain develops.

The following principles governed the procedure:

- The passages chosen must be worth reading.
- There must be a problem solving aspect to the activity that is challenging but does not permit failure.
- The children would be asked to manipulate or work directly on the text in some way – children play and experiment with spoken language (Weir 1962), but they are rarely, except for the Breakthrough to Literacy materials, permitted to play with written language – to provide opportunities for the development of metalinguistic awareness (Cazden 1983).

The design of this study is naturalistic with the focus on the learning phenomenon itself (Teale 1982), with reader–text interactions, and the researcher in the role of participant observer (Harste 1982), in a curriculum development enquiry. Natural texts were used as recommended by Goodman and Gespass (1983) as a result of their study of children's miscues on pronouns in natural texts compared with their performance on specially constructed texts which tended to lack the linguistic complexity of natural texts.

The work was carried out for one hour a week over the equivalent of two half terms in a small rural Cambridgeshire primary school. The nine children of 10–11 years of age and, according to their teacher, of average or above average ability, were chosen by her as a group that would benefit from work on reading development. As a class, they were used to group work and to parents, teachers or students working alongside the class teacher. Therefore the work was carried out in a naturalistic setting within their own classroom. The texts were chosen to conform with the principles outlined in the introduction to this section.

Each child was given a copy of the text under discussion and opportunities provided for individual, paired and group reading within each session; the normal pattern being group leader reads aloud, children read individually and attempt to solve the problem. They then compare their responses in pairs justifying their choice by reference to the text and finally this is repeated with the group as a whole.

In the short term the results showed that the children were enthusiastic about the approach and a bank of materials was built up for use in the class group study. That the children did draw on information from beyond the sentence boundaries can be seen in the following examples where the discussion was tape-recorded:

> In the war, too, were laid the seeds of another great chapter in the story of motoring, Frank Whittle's work on jet engines for aeroplanes was later to lead to the development of the world's first turbine cars. And it was the Rover company who played a big part in this too. During the war, they worked with Whittle on his aero engines. When —— came, they found themselves possessed of a great deal of knowledge concerning gas turbine engines.

The word deleted is peace, part of the lexical chain war in line one, war in line four and then peace the antonym in line five. This was part of the discussion where there is justification of choice of word by reference to the text across a sentence boundary:

Children: I put peace.
                I put they.
                I put they.
                I put they.

Researcher: When they came?
When peace came?
Any other suggestions?
Child: It
Child: I've got 'When peace came', after the war.

Evidence from across the sentence boundary is also presented in this example:

In a pother of dust by no means to Frau Wolff's liking (she was rolling pastry), the bags were dumped on the kitchen floor. She made them take them into the yard. —— out they staggered with their burdens.

The word deleted is 'So' a causal conjunction.

Children: So
So
And
Then
Then
Then
It could be 'Then' or 'So'.
'Well out they staggered with their'
I put 'So out they staggered'
It could be 'Then' or 'Now' or 'So'
It's what they're going to do.
Researcher: Yes it's what's happening next isn't it?
Child: What did he (the writer) use?
Researcher: In fact . . .
Child: It could be 'Then'. It could be 'Now'. It could be 'So'.
Child S: I think 'So' is better.
Child: I think 'Now' is better.
Researcher: You think that 'So' is better. Why?
Child S: She was telling them to take them out and *so* they did.

Replacing deleted conjunctions seems to be a particularly useful teaching activity and one which, according to Leonardi (1981) also proves beneficial for those reading English as a second language. During the sequencing activities this group made very good use of lexical and reference links in sequencing passages, but relatively little use of conjunctions.

So interested were the children that indirect attention to cohesive ties and chains could be moved to explicit direction to their existence and role, as illustrated in the following examples. It will be noted that direct teaching of the use of cohesive ties did *not* involve the use of language drill exercises, nor the use of skills training removed from other learning activities. In fact, one approach is to look at the good practice of successful writers. This can also serve as a 'taster' session for a book that the group, or individual children may want to read for themselves, as in the following example:

Prologue

The sun shines into a large, comfortable room where a family of six, four children and two adults, is having breakfast. It is Sunday morning. 'Why, she's done it, then,' exclaims the father of the family, looking up from his newspaper.

'Who's done what, Dad?' asks the oldest child, a boy.

'Rosie. My friend Rosie. Listen. This is what they've got here. Dr Rosie Angela Lee has been nominated for the Nobel Peace Prize for her work with children in need throughout the world . . .' He pauses, 'Good old Rosie.'

'That's the one who sent me that super book at Christmas,' announces the youngest child, through a large quantity of jam.

'Yes, that's the one,' says her mother, removing some of the jam. 'Your father's first girl friend.'

'Why didn't you marry her, then?' asks the stroppy one, the second.

'She wouldn't have him,' says their mother.

'Well, she wouldn't have anyone else, either. But I tell you one thing.'

'You're always telling us one thing, Dad' says the stroppy one, bored.

'Sh,' says his mother.

'If it hadn't been for Rosie, you probably wouldn't be here now, and I would be in gaol, I suspect . . .'

'Not you, Dad. You've always been one of the goodies . . .'

'Little do you know. Why, come to think of it. I must have been one of the first of those to receive the benefit of Rosie Angela Lee.'

The passage was read through silently, then the researcher read the passage aloud and discussed the nature of a prologue, with particular emphasis on the need to set the scene and introduce characters. The characters and identity chains were traced one by one, using a different colour to identify each character. These were compared in pairs and then in the group as a whole; so there was explicit direction followed by interactive discussion.

The problem-solving challenge was to find and trace the identity chains within the text, but this was set within the wider problem faced by the writer in introducing and distinguishing the characters.

All members of the group were able to resolve most of the cohesive ties in the identity chains. The more able in the group realized that *family*, *adults* and *children* and then individuals were introduced. The only point where there was agreement to differ was the resolution of 'you' in line 18. 'If it hadn't been for Rosie, you probably wouldn't be here now . . .'

They suggested that 'you' could refer to 'the stroppy one', who had just spoken, or to all the children, or to all the children and their mother. For one member of the group this depended on the interpretation of the demonstrative reference item 'here' which to him meant 'alive' or 'have been born' rather than more literally 'in this place' (i.e. the family kitchen)

and therefore excluded mother from you. It was suggested that the interpretation would depend on the individual family and probably would be
resolved only by reading the rest of the story.

The following strategies for distinguishing characters were identified
by the group:

1. The use of lexical collocates 'family', 'adults', 'children' to assist the
   structure of the passage.
2. Alongside this was the use of numbers, allowing the writer to omit any
   further reference to one of the children.
3. 'Mother' is always referred to as 'mother' never as 'she' in order to avoid
   confusion with 'Rosie', the only other adult, female character.
4. The children were labelled with subtitles 'the oldest one', the youngest
   one', 'the stroppy one', using demonstrative reference 'the' and nominal substitute 'one' in each case.

Other activities directing awareness to cohesive ties and chains consisted of
circling demonstrative items and drawing arrows to what they 'point to';
grouping words together that seem to 'go together' in some way and then
predict what the passage is about that they came from; grouping connectives together in families with a similar meaning and then attempting to use
some that they had not used before.

A criticism of the approach, that has been outlined, might be that
good writing should not be used in this manner. However, in an essay on
style Enkvist (1964) describes two sorts of readers as two sorts of onlookers
at a magician's performance; those who sit back and enjoy the wonder of
the magician's art, and those who want to know how the tricks are carried
out. It is argued in this book that an appreciation of how the writing is
'done' enhances rather than detracts from the wonder and the pleasure of
the reader.

Further evidence of the value of the activity came from the class teacher's interest in the work being carried out, in her conviction that it did
carry over into other aspects of the curriculum, and her own use and
development of the approach after the study ended. Two years after the
end of this study the researcher made a videotaped programme of the
teacher's work in this area, for use in teacher education courses.

A class study

This was a study of two class groups of children. One class had specific
teaching related to the perception of cohesive ties in continuous text while
the other class group did not. Comparisons were made between the groups'
performances on a reading pre-test and post-test. A before and after control

group design was employed, where both groups were tested at the same time and were assigned to groups and to treatments randomly, after the pre-test. The independent variable was teaching related to the perception of cohesive ties in continuous text. The dependent variable was reading ability as measured by performance on Edinburgh Reading Test Stage 3.

The sample consisted of 62, 10- or 11-year-old children from two classes of vertically grouped third and fourth year children in a rural/ suburban Hertfordshire school. The Edinburgh Reading Test was chosen because, although time consuming to administer, it provides a range of different reading tasks and a variety of different types of texts. This is unusual in standardized group reading tests. The materials used for teaching were those, or based on those, developed during the small group study.

The control treatment consisted of language work – prediction, drawing, discussion of development of plot and characters and writing related to the story – linked to one book, a lively novel which proved very popular with the group, i.e. *Gowie Corby Plays Chicken*, by Gene Kemp.

The experimental treatment consisted of: identifying identity chains in passages, commenting on the use of pronouns in place of names, identifying strategies used by writers for coping with potential ambiguity; cloze tasks involving replacing deleted cohesive items and supporting one's choice by reference to evidence in the text; drawing arrows from demonstratives to show what they point to; group sequencing of stories; grouping words together about the same topic; and choosing alternative conjunctions. In addition this group had one chapter of *Gowie Corby Plays Chicken* read to them each week.

The study was carried out for one afternoon a week over a summer term. With time for testing and the usual summer term interruptions, this left eight sessions for teaching. Each group came for either the first or last half of the afternoon session, the order alternating weekly. All the teaching was carried out by the researcher in a spare classroom.

The results on the reading pre-test and post-test are presented in Table 5. Using a 't' test, the difference between the means is not statistically significant. Therefore the teaching did not appear to make a significant difference to the experimental group, even though the mean score for the experimental group was higher.

The results are not quite as clear cut as Table 5 might suggest. There were several weaknesses in this study. Although the children and the treatments were assigned to groups randomly, the experimental group was more demanding to work with, containing one child with behaviour difficulties. Since it was the researcher herself who did both sets of teaching there was in fact teacher awareness of cohesive patterning for both groups. The researcher was also aware of which was the experimental group and was more anxious during those sessions. With such brief contact over eight

Table 5   Mean scores on Edinburgh Reading Test Stage 3, on occasion 1 and on occasion 2 for the experimental group (teaching about cohesion) and for the control group (no teaching about cohesion)

	Occasion 1	*Occasion 2*
Experimental group	mean score 87.41	mean score 94.31
	n = 29	n = 29
Control group	mean score 87.85	mean score 92.15
	n = 27	n = 27

sessions it might have been better to have worked with smaller groups, or to have allowed a longer preparatory period to have established group work with the children. In retrospect it was unfortunate that all the work carried out was with narrative texts, to keep the experience of the two groups as similar as possible. The experimental group might have benefited from some work with non-narrative texts. The small group study had in fact used narrative and non-narrative passages and this was perceived by the class teacher as advantageous. Indeed the Edinburgh Reading Test Stage 3 does consist of both narrative and non-narrative texts but non-narrative pre-dominate. This need to focus on non-narrative texts was discussed with and successfully followed up by Winchester in her 1984 study.

Summary

The limited impact of earlier models of reading on classroom practice was reviewed. It was argued that, on the whole, schools, until very recently, had done little to develop reading beyond the initial stages. It was stressed that in fluent reading it is necessary to have a knowledge of written language as well as of subject matter.

The notion of cohesion was introduced and studies of cohesion and reading were reviewed. Comprehension was seen to be central to this model of reading and a study of the relationship between ability to replace items deleted from cohesive chains and comprehension was examined. The findings of that study suggested that there is a relationship between the two. Previous knowledge did not seem to make a great deal of difference to these able readers.

Insights from the model of reading were incorporated into a teaching programme and two examples of its implementation were presented. The need for greater use of non-narrative texts in such a programme was identified.

Overall, it is important to realize that apparent ability to understand structures and usage in spoken language does not necessarily transfer to understanding these structures and usage in written texts in a range of registers.

CHAPTER 4

Teaching and developing reading in this changing context

Reading – a new definition

A new definition of reading development then must take some account of the extended reading of complete and sometimes complex texts and acknowledge the influence of having read one text on one's reading of another text. It must take on board the power of discussion and interaction in the development of reading and consider a much wider range of reading settings than simply the textbook or the reading scheme book. An invaluable resource and source of motivation for this can be out of school demands and experience. The emphasis should be not on teaching method but on learning strategy. All of this must be seen as embedded in the social and cultural expectations of children, family, community and government, at the tail end of the twentieth century.

Strategies for reading whole texts

One of the challenges of reading a whole text is getting to the end. That may require some stamina, an area of reading development which has tended to be rather neglected because it can be time consuming in an already overloaded curriculum. The following can help in this situation: the provision of opportunities for uninterrupted, silent reading; the careful monitoring and targeting of resources to children making the transition from reading short stories and beginning to read longer stories with chapters; the closer involvement of the home; the use of paired reading and taped stories. The following general points may also be worth considering:

1. Expect the content to be related to the title.
2. From the title predict the type of words that might occur. That is, build up a semantic net of related words. Consider opposites, synonyms, words that refer to groups, to parts or to wholes.
3. If the content is not related to the title or heading why has that happened? Is it for a special effect? Is it because it isn't a good title? Is it because the passage isn't well written? Not every text used in schools is well written and we do our pupils no service by allowing them to assume that they are.
4. Expect to find a beginning, a middle and an end. If this pattern does not occur why is that? Is there another pattern?
5. If an argument is presented identify it and mark or note the supporting evidence. What is the conclusion? Does this conclusion follow from the evidence presented? Are any reservations expressed in the text? Are there any which you think should be expressed?
6. Does the information reinforce your own observations or experiences or information from other sources including other texts?
7. What have you learned about the writer by reading the text?

Strategies for reading complex texts

The strategies in the previous section may also be used. In addition, it may be useful to employ the following:

1. Look carefully at the connectives, particularly those that link sentences. Are the relationships in meaning between the sentences clear?
2. Sometimes the order in which sentences are presented implies a relationship. Does this occur in this passage?
3. If the vocabulary is unfamiliar this may be because unfamiliar synonyms or antonyms are being used. In this case a thesaurus may be useful.
4. If the text is impenetrable because of the content try a simpler introductory text on the same subject.
5. When in doubt resort to reading aloud, the intonation pattern may help to clarify meaning. Most fluent readers use this strategy on occasion.

Shared reading (Figure 2)

As pointed out in the foreword to a companion volume to this (E. Anderson 1988), in reviewing research on reading in 1977 Moseley and Moseley refer to the evidence then available that children's reading and language performance benefit where: 'home and school support each other in progress towards mutually understood and agreed goals' (1977: 66). Since that

Figure 2   We enjoy sharing books

date further evidence has proliferated (Tizard *et al.* 1982, Topping and Wolfendale 1985, Swinson 1986) and there are shared reading and parental involvement projects all over the country.

Such an approach is not easy, but rests essentially on mutual trust, agreement and understanding.

The reason for the success of shared reading and its spread at this time is because it is consonant with our increased awareness and understanding of the development of children's language and learning and also with our understanding of the nature of literacy.

It is now accepted that language is complex, and that it develops through interaction with someone else, when both participants are attending to and share an interest in the same subject or object. It is also accepted that the role of parents and other adults is central to children's development (Tizard *et al.* 1981).

Similarly, Donaldson's (1978) work has noted the benefits of children working together on problems. This in turn has increased teachers' awareness of children's pre-school learning (Paley 1981) and has encouraged an increase in collaborative learning activities between children and between adults.

At the same time there has been an increasing awareness of the nature of literacy and its development before school. It is now clear that most children come to school with a developing concept of story (Applebee 1978), with a sense that the language of books is different from everyday language (Clark 1976). Children in our society do not meet print for the first time when they enter school; they grow up surrounded by print in shops, on labels and on television and they have their own ideas about how it works (Clay 1972, Goodman 1984, Ferreiro 1985).

Even at secondary school level, group reading and discussion activities have proved a powerful means of learning (Davies and Greene 1984) and as Lunzer and Gardner discovered:

> learning is enhanced when more than one language mode is employed . . . When they are used together in the same setting, reading may provide the stimulus to thinking; spoken language gives it reality and sustains it; finally, writing crystallizes the product. (1979: 313)

Shared reading fits into this overall pattern by contributing to the continuity of experience for the child from home to school. It is about sharing complete meaningful texts, whether story or information. In the sharing the gap may be bridged between spoken and written language because there is a voice to listen to and a face to look at. Gradually the child is able to take on the rhythms and patterns of continuous written texts without losing the sense of what is being read and at the same time builds up expectations and predictions about different types of text. Such is the basis of fluent reading. Sharing a book continues the process of language development that started at birth. Sharing a book allows opportunities to talk about writing and language itself (Cazden 1983). It allows consideration of style and of the person who wrote the book (E. Anderson 1983a). In our increasingly complex society we require adults and children who not only read the written word but who question it. Sharing a book allows for mismatches or misunderstandings of, for example, social or cultural settings (Steffensen 1981, E. Anderson 1984b) to be made explicit.

The obvious extension of shared reading then is shared writing. Such an approach relies heavily on parents', teachers' and librarians' knowledge of books. There are increasing numbers of excellent books being produced and only detailed knowledge of these will enable adults to support and monitor the continuing development of children's facility with written language throughout all of the school years.

Further practical suggestions for introducing shared reading to colleagues, parents and children are contained in Davis and Stubbs (1988).

Reading for real (Figures 3 and 4)

Thanks to the work of Harrison (1980), Lunzer and Gardner (1979), Davies and Greene (1984) and Morris and Stewart-Dore (1984), as teachers we are much more aware of the reading demands of textbooks and curriculum materials used in school. However, we do not have the same control of *real life* materials from sources outside the school. One of the central arguments of this book is that education should be perceived as a continuous process from birth to death. There should be no discontinuity on entry to or on leaving the school system. The case for using materials from outside school is then self-evident, logically, motivationally and educationally. So lack of control of the levels of difficulty of such materials should not be sufficient cause for abandoning their use.

What are the materials that can be used in such a way and what are the problems? The work of Goodman (1984) and of Ferreiro (1985) has illustrated that children coming into school bring with them an awareness and knowledge of print in their environment. This may be from such diverse sources as advertising, street signs and computer games. All of this can be replicated and built upon in the classroom and on field trips by the incorporation and exploitation of print in as many forms and functions as possible. In the teacher's forward planning all that is required is the addition of another column with the heading public print. In the past such an approach would have been considered problematic because of the range of print styles presented. However, children do not seem to find such variation as dificult as adults would have predicted. What is essential is that the print occurs in a context which makes the meaning and function clear.

Figure 3   Using the school log book to find out about school in wartime

Figure 4   Reading and checking the school concert accounts

Yetta Goodman (1984) found pre-school children who could not 'read' the name of a hamburger chain but could tell her from the print in an advertisement that they were not allowed to eat there.

In local history studies we are encouraged to make use of local newspapers, but the style of even 50 years ago may be much more demanding than we had anticipated. Indeed, if the newspapers were published during the Second World War the source of much of the material might well be reports from government departments. As an example two leaders from the same local paper are contrasted, one from a 1939 edition and one from 1990.

Huntly Express

Huntly, September 1, 1939

Preparedness

It may be said with truth that Great Britain has never before in peace-time been so well prepared for any emergency. Our regular forces are far larger and far more fully equipped, thanks to the excellent recruiting of the past year and the effort of the departments to make service more attractive and efficient. The organisation of Civil Defence, too, has had a great moral effect. We have reason to believe that the dangers arising from air raids can be minimised, now that two million volunteers will know what to do if war comes. Shelters have been provided for the workers and the unwanted adults and children will leave the town for the country. Evacuation of these people from certain areas commenced this morning and emergency rations are already at the various reception points throughout the country. Aberdeenshire is well prepared to receive up to 40,000 children from the Glasgow area, and all arrangements for telephonic communication with reception officers, the appointment of assistants for reception and billeting, the provision of hot meals to the children on arrival, and the conveyance of evacuees to beyond two miles of the reception are completed. The effect has been to give us all confidence. And the prompt passage of the Emergency Powers (Defence) Act and the readiness of the Government to use it, as, for example, in placing all merchantmen under the orders of the Admiralty, have confirmed the belief that all has been done that can be done to make ready for any sudden adverse change in the situation.

Those who remember the critical days of July–August 1914 or the agitated week at the end of last September will know that things were very different then. In 1914 and in 1938 there was widespread anxiety that is not discoverable now. Ever since Munich we have watched with keen interest and approval the Government's steady efforts to strengthen the country in every possible way. We have been permitted to know that reserves of foodstuffs and raw materials were being amassed, and the prospects of a good average harvest that are now being realised confirm the belief that our people will have enough to eat, whatever happens. We are far better off than Germany, where rationing was announced on Sunday. Our financial position is immensely strong and has been buttressed against shocks by the decision to let sterling find its own gold level and by the banning of the sale abroad of foreign securities. It is far better that all such precautionary measures should have been taken well in advance of the emergency, which, if it should come, will find us calm and ready.

Huntly Express

Friday, 2nd November, 1990

A test of education

SCOTLAND may be justly proud of her education process which, through the centuries, has been painstakingly built up so that everyone may have the same education as everyone else. It is free and it is equal for everyone.

Most educationalists agree that, especially in its primary departments, it is pretty good. Whatever is wrong, it is claimed by those most involved, could best be put right by having more resources put into the system. Money is the key.

Education minister, Michael Forsyth, would not agree. Instead of quelling the restless natives, he wants to start a revolution.

First, it was school boards. He thought by giving guns to the parents they could shoot the restless teachers. What has happened? Instead of wanting more say in what is taught, the parent-members are backing the teachers and clamouring for more resources themselves.

Second, it was 'opting out'. Instead of leaving the country to the natives (and others naïve enough to stay) only one school board has shown any interest in opting out, and even they have now withdrawn.

SO MR FORSYTH DANGLES THE CARROT OF A CASH DEAL IF THEY WILL PLEASE DO AS HE SAYS AND OPT OUT.

Third, what can only be a rehash of the old Eleven Plus examination in all but name. So far, the only people who seem to want official testing like this are Messrs Rifkind and Forsyth.

Is it a case of, if you can't beat the natives, neither do you have to join them? A first and second class system in the classroom might be better than nothing.

Fourth, when all else fails, offer a bribe in the form of a voucher to get away from it all – presumably to a private school, since education in normal schools is free.

Why all this?

DO YOU THINK IT IS FOR THE GOOD OF EDUCATION IN SCOTLAND?

The contrasts between the two pieces of writing are obvious. The 1939 passage is longer (by 125 words); the sentences are longer (by eleven point seven words on average; more polysyllabic words are used (on average by twenty-seven syllables per hundred words); archaic forms are used such as 'telephonic communication' and 'conveyance'. In addition, there is little use of explicit connection in the 1939 passage. The only examples are: 'too' in the third sentence, 'And' half way through the passage. Whereas the structure of the 1990 passage is quite explicit with the use of 'First', 'Second', 'Third', 'Fourth' preceded on three occasions by 'Instead' and accompanied by 'So'.

The coherence of the 1939 passage is achieved by the use of comparison, for example 'better' and 'more' in the second sentence and 'such' in the final sentence; by the use of ellipsis 'The effect' near the middle of the passage; and by use of nominal reference using 'we' and 'our' referring back to 'Great Britain' in the first sentence. Collocation is used rather than the more straightforward reiteration and on the whole the distance between items in the chains is greater and the reference tends to be to groups of words rather than to single items.

In the 1990 passage coherence is achieved explicitly by the reiteration of 'Scotland' which appears as first and last word in the passage; by the use of two main chains using nominal reference and reiteration one containing 'Scotland' and the other 'education'. The style of the two passages differs, and the children did find the 1939 passage challenging and required help in understanding why this was so. While working on the same project on the Second World War, the following difficulty was encountered in reading a report of the results of local football matches. The interest of the item was that at that time there were four or five teams in an area where there is now not a single football team. The source of the difficulty was the following example of ellipsis:

> Matches have been played between teams representing Balnoon and Auchaber. Auchaber were victorious. In the first game the scores were Auchaber 5 Balnoon 1: in the return game Auchaber 4 Balnoon 1. (*Huntly Express* 1 September 1939)

The problem with no verb (ellipsis) in the final statement was identified when one girl found it difficult to find an appropriate intonation pattern when attempting to read it aloud, as part of a dramatic production about the area during the Second World War. She summed the situation up by declaring that she couldn't read it because she didn't understand it.

Reading from the reader's viewpoint

It is now almost 29 years since the publication of Reid's (1966) seminal work on young children's concept of reading and it has borne valuable fruit in terms of early years practice. But do we really address the question of reading purpose with older pupils? If we don't then how can we evaluate reading collaboratively or effectively? How can we assess their achievements? It is only with the reader's own self-evaluation that further development may be achieved. It is from the areas of adult literacy and of the development of assessment strategies for standard grade (Fyfe and Mitchell 1985) that we have had the most valuable insights in this respect. In particular, Good and Holmes (1978) in the Adult Literacy Unit booklet *How's it Going? an alternative to testing students in adult literacy* provided a framework for assessment through partnership rather than a tutor imposed test. The first question in that framework is 'Do you use reading with a sense of purpose? For real things you need like TV guides, labels, etc., as well as just wanting to learn to read?'

Reading and information handling

The use of hardware alone does not ensure development in literacy as all teachers know, who have watched children mindlessly pressing the space bar to get on to the next frame or pressing keys at random. Certainly this builds up confidence which must be a pre-requisite but confidence is only valuable when it is accompanied by awareness of the task in hand and knowledge of the potential as well as the limitations of the hardware and software available.

The problem with information accessing skills in the past has been that instruction is most effective when there is a genuine question to be answered which can be answered from the available resources. This brings to mind a classroom with multiple copies of a very simple dictionary and the explanation of a child in that class that he didn't use a dictionary because the words he wanted weren't in the dictionary. A range of information must be available to provide for progression in this area as much as any other. The same applies to databases.

As with printed paper texts children learn from the behaviour modelled by their teachers. How much school information is stored on disc?

Another problem of accessing information has been the use of indexes. Key words are a useful but limited tool. How useful is 'sheep' in the index if the word being searched for is 'ewe'? In this respect work on lexical relationships such as meronomy can prove useful in helping the children to generate a range of related terms when they are trying to use an index or contents list. At the end of the day it must be remembered, as Fyfe and Mitchell's (1988) research has demonstrated, many children's books are not sufficiently well constructed in this respect to support the development of accessing skills. Fyfe and Mitchell's (1988) study of the assessment of inquiry reading is particularly noteworthy, covering as it does areas such as planning, searching, recording and editing in a practical and manageable manner.

However, perhaps the most valuable exercise is for the children to construct contents lists and indexes for their own work. Many of those presented in school textbooks provide poor models for the children.

Reading for all – supporting reading and learning across the curriculum

Reading is a right for all children. Many will find it relatively easy and the main task of the teacher will be to ensure and check progression (Davis and

Stubbs 1988: 65–72; profile is useful in this respect) and the provision and availability of appropriate resources, experiences and opportunities. However, progression and development in reading in all the curriculum areas must also be monitored. There are particular dificulties with maths texts, as Rothery (1983) has demonstrated. There are problems with the use of technical vocabulary and the related problem of using everyday language such as 'half', 'similar' or 'difference' in a much more precise and technical manner. Writers of maths texts have a tendency to use a rather formal academic style which may introduce grammatical difficulties. Mathematics makes a great deal of use of symbols, and these are not necessarily read from left to right. The written language is often linked to diagrams or other visual material which may have to be read in a different way as in the use of graphs. Rothery also points out that there may be several different styles of writing on one page of a maths textbook since the different parts of the page may have different purposes such as explanation, statement, instruction as well as providing exercises.

Gardner (1977, 1983) has drawn attention to the development of children's full understanding of logical connectives such as 'thus', 'therefore' and 'however'. He found that understanding of these is not complete until well into the secondary school. I remember vividly an able 11-year-old girl who argued vehemently that 'therefore' meant exactly the same as 'then'. When one considers it one can comprehend this partial understanding. Often 'therefore' comes at the end of a list of occurrences, so frequently it does signal the end point in a time sequence. This girl could use 'then' and 'therefore' in a grammatically and seemingly a semantically appropriate manner but without realizing the full logical import of 'therefore'. Awareness of this on the part of the researcher occurred only during a group reading and discussion session when the problem posed was to choose alternative conjunctions for a passage.

Reading strategies specific to science texts have been identified by Davies and Greene (1984). The approaches are similar to those group reading and discussion activities discussed in the teaching programme in Chapter 3, but they tailor them to science texts that are widely used in schools.

The general strategies for developing reading across the curriculum derive from the work of Lunzer and Gardner (1979) using group reading and discussion with prediction, sequencing, text marking and cloze activities.

Less well known is an Australian approach known as ERICA – Effective Reading in Content Areas (Morris and Stewart-Dore 1984). They identify four stages in reading for learning:

1. Preparing for reading.
2. Thinking through the reading.

3. Extracting and organizing information.
4. Translating information.

A very useful summary of this work and examples of its application in a British school has been provided by Jennifer Eden (1991).

Reading for the future

In order to cope in a changing world it is necessary to approach reading as a problem solving or problem tackling activity. As Fyfe and Mitchell (1985) point out, in the past our assessment of reading and comprehension has assumed that there is only one right answer to questions. Many years ago a colleague summed up the problems some students were having understanding a piece of research, by saying that they had a low toleration of ambiguity. Traditionally our education system has not always valued or prepared children for coping with ambiguity. Perhaps our system of examining postgraduate degrees in education has not helped in this respect, encouraging for the sake of the development of an argument the dismissal of alternative interpretations through a polarization of viewpoints. Educationists in the twentieth century, with their creation of these false dichotomies are hardly shining examples of good practice. The encouragement of collaborative learning, of group discussion activities, of the sifting, analysis and synthesis of information from different sources and viewpoints, of the imaginative use of role play and drama, of adults learning alongside children, all help to counteract this tendency. But an ability to tolerate ambiguity requires confidence in one's own abilities, skill in reading and understanding information, a willingness to listen and consider alternative viewpoints and a set of beliefs and values against which to make judgements. Such activities and development would seem to be at the heart of education and a necessary part of personal, social and moral development as well as an integral part of responding to both the complexity and the simplicity of the arts.

The seeds of such development are sown before school and should be cultivated throughout, though the demands of this on the teacher are enormous. Thank goodness for the Simons of this world who jolt us out of our preconceptions, not to mention ruts. On his first day at school Simon was asked to colour some apples red. After several requests there was still no sign of activity. The teacher was pretty sure that he knew his colours but stayed around to investigate further. At last Simon posed the problem. 'But what if they were Golden Delicious? They wouldn't be red then.' The teacher agreed but pointed out that there was a written instruction 'Colour the apples red'. Suitably impressed by his teacher's reading ability and proud of his ability to identify the word 'red', Simon completed the activity.

But that has not stopped him questioning activities that conflict with his view of the world or asking questions that begin 'But what if . . .?' Few of his questions have one clear-cut answer.

Professional communication about reading

There would appear to be very few people who are not capable of learning to read, given the opportunity and appropriate support and resources. One of the dangers of our overloaded curriculum is that the opportunities have to be safeguarded and planned for. The chief HMI for primary education in England and Wales has recently expressed concern that time for reading development is being eroded in schools. Parents have expressed the view that time is being spent testing reading when it could more appropriately be spent on teaching and developing reading. So alongside the sound theoretical arguments for increasing parental involvement and shared reading we must also consider its contribution to the management of that most expensive and valuable resource, teacher time.

The professional education of teachers this century has encouraged and continues to encourage students and teachers to be self-critical. This is quite appropriate, but only if it is accompanied by confidence and feelings of worth both professionally and individually which can be communicated to children, parents and the wider community. The training institutions have been far more successful with the former than the latter. But that is no wonder when we look at the changes and pressures that they have had to face and meet since the Robbins Report of the early 1960s.

Teaching children to read and monitoring their development is one of the most rewarding aspects of teaching. Do we share our enthusiasm and delight about this with our pupils and their families or are we so tired and anxious by the time that parental consultations come round that we are tempted to stress the problems rather than the successes? Unfortunately reading does not usually leave a permanent record that can be put in a pupil file or taken out and displayed to parents, so it is all the more important that we ensure that parents are able to share in their children's reading development right across the curriculum.

The final chapter of this book deals with the communication of such matters in much greater detail.

Summary

It was argued that reading development must take account of:

- The extended reading of complete and sometimes complex texts.
- The power of discussion.

- The importance of interaction.
- The need to consider a wider range of materials and settings for reading.
- The expectations of children, families and community.

Issues related to teaching and developing reading in this changing context were addressed. These included strategies for reading whole texts; strategies for reading complex texts; shared reading; reading materials drawn from the real world; looking at reading from the reader's viewpoint; information handling; supporting reading and learning across the curriculum; reading to meet the demands of the future; and professional communication about reading.

CHAPTER 5

Teaching reading within national curricula

Introduction

It is argued in this chapter that the theoretical framework presented in this book and the practical strategies recommended are entirely consonant with the requirements of the national curriculum documents in Scotland, England and Wales. The two documents are examined and commented on in slightly different ways. This reflects the writer's own use of the documents, for one her role as reader is mainly as a teacher, for the other it is as an examiner of teacher education courses. But the difference in style of response also reflects the differing styles of the two documents, one is a working paper, the other is a legal document and consequently the less formal one is more user friendly.

Scotland

In the rationale of the Scottish Education Department (SED) document *English Language 5–14* (1990) it is acknowledged that:

- Children's earliest language is acquired in the home, and schools will build on that foundation.
- That language will mirror the diversity of the community the school serves and contribute to the learning that occurs in the classroom.
- Hence this language will require to be handled with respect if confidence is to be built up.

It is also recommended that schools should provide structured and stimulating opportunities to use language with increasing precision in contexts appropriate to the needs of individuals and the world in which they live. This will involve communicating, thinking, feeling and making.

It is suggested that language work can best be structured by referring to what the Working Paper describes as the 'main features of language – Listening, Talking, Reading and Writing – and the purposes for which they are normally used.' In this context 'features' would seem to be an inappropriate usage and should be replaced by 'modes'. Nevertheless, the general point is taken that language must be viewed as a whole, but the modes do differ and should also be considered separately. As with so many areas of education it can be argued that there should be a core course where the subject or curriculum area is understood, alongside permeation and full and meaningful integration. Otherwise the pupils are faced with cognitive confusion of the type described by Downing (1979) and by Valtin (1986) and which may be at the root of many specific language difficulties.

The general point is made that a knowledge of purposes, a sense of audience, in a rich variety of contexts 'improves language skills and allows learners to gauge more effectively their own progress and achievements'. The emphasis then is on self-evaluation and monitoring.

The aims for language teaching and learning are wide ranging and sensitive to the special place of language in the development of self-concept as well as independence and personal development.

Within the specific issues discussed it is stressed, as would be expected, that problems with language development can usually be overcome by an appropriate curriculum and methodology and that by identifying, assessing and responding to such needs in a planned and systematic way the school can provide access to language that is the right of all pupils.

It is also particularly pleasing to see that this document does address fully the social and cultural context in which language is used and develops. Alongside this, it is argued that all children need a knowledge about language and a vocabulary to talk about language in order to extend their implicit knowledge of language, thus supplementing but not subverting the normal processes of language acquisition.

It raises issues of equal opportunities for the sexes, the importance of Scottish culture and language and the school's duty to develop awareness of this diversity 'helping pupils to value themselves and their own beliefs while respecting and valuing the beliefs and rights of others'.

The approaches touched on in the rationale are the use of mass media, computers and drama.

Overall then the rationale does appear to acknowledge the learning and ways of knowing that children bring with them to school; the increasingly complex literacy demands of modern technological society; the importance of group interaction; and the need for educating all. Language is viewed as communication and the importance of the social and cultural setting to its development is accepted.

What is presented in the working paper, it is claimed, is a framework to ensure balance, continuity, coherence and progression; a framework consisting of attainment targets, programmes of study and a structure for assessment and recording.

The following *outcome* in reading is identified:

> Pupils will read, on occasion aloud, to enjoy and respond to a variety of texts, finding and handling information for a range of purposes; in so doing, they will achieve an awareness of genre and knowledge about language. (SED 1990: 9)

Within the attainment targets for reading there are seven strands: close reading, reading aloud, reading for information, reading for enjoyment, finding and handling information, awareness of genre and knowledge about language.

There are a number of statements made on specific issues which are relevant to the present discussion.

Special educational needs are approached in a positive and constructive manner stressing adaptation of the programme of study to the needs of the child, and the importance of co-operation between teachers, specialists, parents and pupils to enable successful learning to take place.

The section on knowledge about language (SED 1990: 19) makes clear that use of language should develop before attempts are made to introduce explicit knowledge, in order to improve performance and extend understanding. Attention is also drawn to the fact that the perception of the manipulation of larger units of language contributes to the development and use of language.

Genre is defined in this document as a term 'used to describe a property of texts, that each text belongs to a group, or set of texts with which it shares common features'.

In fact, in the context of this document 'genre' seems to bear some relation to the use of 'register' in this book.

Broad genres are presented as for example prose, poetry and drama. These can be subdivided further, e.g. prose into fiction and non-fiction; and fiction for example into romance, horror, science fiction, detective story; and non-fiction for example into journalism, works of history, astronomy, etc. However, perhaps the clearest description of genre and its relationship to register is made in the *Times Educational Supplement* (*Scotland*) of 29 March 1991 in 'The School Diaries of Morris Simpson, M.A.' series in the excerpt entitled 'Gazumped by my own genre'. The ill-fated teacher of English sees the effectiveness of his teaching with regard to the 'estate agent advertisement' genre when on the first day of the holidays he reads an advertisement which is a glowing description, in the appropriate genre, of a property which fits the description of his school!

For alternative teaching strategies and a thorough discussion of the topic see another volume in this series, *Reading All Types of Writing* (Littlefair 1991).

On a more serious note, the SED document goes on to justify genre as an area of concern as it is claimed that a sense of genre brings with it an awareness of the appropriateness of the language used for its purpose, content and audience, and facilitates making predictions, skimming, scanning and identifying the gist of a text. They go on to claim that this aids effective communication. Therefore, where such skill does not develop readily, awareness of genre should be deliberately and consciously taught.

The issue of gender inequality is presented with reference to the choice of resources, the importance of modelling behaviour within the school, the construction of groups and the open discussion of such matters with pupils.

A positive approach and attitude is advocated in the respect for and maintenance of linguistic and cultural diversity. This section ends with the very important caveat:

> The school and the pupil must work together towards early achievement of the targets in English. However, the overall ability of learners should not be judged solely by their command of English, which may, by necessity, be incomplete. (SED 1990: 21)

In the section on Scottish culture it is stated that Scottish writing and writing about Scotland should permeate the curriculum and be introduced from an early stage. The purpose is to value and critically examine the ideas, beliefs and emotions of Scottish writers, and set them against the different insights and perspectives of writers from other places and other times.

Because children spend more time watching television than they spend in school it is argued that the study of media should be part of the curriculum to enable them to increase their understanding, critical appreciation and enjoyment of the mass media, and to give them a sense of discrimination. The points made that are relevant to reading centre mainly on the use and production of newspapers. Links with the outside world are made explicit in relation to the observation that studying media offers a natural way of investigating texts, discussing personal and social issues and relating to pupils' out of school interests.

It is stated that the key uses of the microcomputer for language development are wordprocessing, desk-top publishing, information handling, adventure games and simulations.

Drama is identified as of central importance in language development.

Throughout the programmes of study in reading the importance of target audience and writer's purpose is stressed. Similarly, the use of public print, instructions and reading which produces action in problem-solving activities are also stressed. Within the strand on reading for enjoyment it is interesting to note the comment that biographical details about poets can help make their work more accessible to pupils. Throughout the present volume knowledge of the writer and the writer's purpose have been stressed. However, the biographical details in some children's books are not particularly reliable and are sometimes misleading. As an example, in only one of the present editions of George MacDonald's children's books are the biographical details correct. The second point of note is the encouragement of teachers reading aloud from non-fiction texts. This is an extremely powerful way into the sometimes complex area of non-fiction texts. In many ways cohesion in written texts has to carry out many of the functions of intonation in spoken texts.

It is in the strands on awareness of genre and knowledge about language that the programmes of study appear to be most similar to the approaches presented in Chapter 3 of this book; while the strategies presented in Chapter 4 are very close to those strands dealing with close reading, reading aloud, reading for information, reading for enjoyment and finding and handling information.

Within the section on assessment it is particularly pleasing to see the following statement with its emphasis on the positive and the constructive: 'Assessment should help to build the confidence necessary to cope with increasing challenge' (SED 1990: 55).

The resource implications identified by the report are in terms of staffing, including staff development. This will be touched on again in Chapter 6.

England and Wales

The corresponding document of the Department of Education and Science (DES) and the Welsh Office is entitled *English in the National Curriculum No. 2* (1990). There is also a schedule with regard to those pupils who have been taught through Welsh in the early years. It is strange that there is no mention of Welsh culture in this section. The attainment targets for English are set out in the profile components to be used for reporting. In the case of Reading these are labelled AT2 and the aim is:

> The development of the ability to read, understand and respond to all types of writing, as well as the development of information-retrieval strategies for the purposes of study. (DES and Welsh Office 1990: 7)

When these targets are examined in terms of the summary of changes presented at the end of Chapter 1 of this volume the following pattern emerges.

A move from the study of small units of language to the study of whole texts

Throughout levels 1–10, i.e. throughout the years of compulsory schooling, and at each level, the references are to stories, to poems and to books. The only references to individual letters, words or phrases occur with the development of phonic skills, the use of dictionaries, the understanding of labels, signs or instructions. It is only at a later stage, level 5, that there is reference to details from the text and that is for use in supporting their own views of the material they read. Indeed there is little progression evident in the development of facility with the smaller units of language. This is surprising in the light of work such as that of Bryant and Bradley (1985) on the importance of early awareness of rhyme and alliteration on reading development.

A move in interest from the study of simple texts to more complex texts

No direct mention is made of text complexity, but the points made in the previous section suggest that what are being recommended are certainly not artificially simplified texts. Indeed from level 7 onwards reference is made to the need to read a range of fiction, poetry, literary non-fiction such as letters, diaries and autobiography, drama, including pre-twentieth century literature, literature in translation and from a range of cultures.

This is reinforced in the programmes of study for reading that suggest ways of tackling increasingly more difficult texts, e.g. using inference, deduction and previous reading experience to go beyond the literal; discussing character, action, fact and opinion; being helped to tackle texts of increasing difficulty.

A move away from the study of isolated individuals to the study of interaction

In the statements of attainment there is no explicit mention of group work. There is, however, mention of role play in the early stages and discussion in the later stages which may imply group work, as well as the reference in level 7 to group presentation and group discussion.

Certainly in the programmes of study there is reference to children reading to each other; participating in shared reading and writing; reading related to play; and discussing books. It is a pity that there is no clearer statement of the value of group work in reading.

*A move from attempts to make the settings of studies of language and
learning as neutral as possible to the use of naturalistic settings*

The first statement in level 1 of the attainment targets in reading makes
reference to the child's awareness that print in the everyday world carries
meaning. It goes on to mention word recognition, but only in familiar
contexts, in role play and in signs, labels, notices and brand names. From
level 3 onwards reading for information is linked with topic work. The wide
range of literary, non-literary and media sources recommended reinforces
the sense of reading being linked to the demands of continuous education
and of the world outside school. Finally there is clear reference to society in
the section on attitudes to language change in our society as represented
by letters to newspapers.

In the programmes of study for Key Stage 1 it is made quite clear that
approaches and materials should reflect the child's experiences outside
school and relate to the real world.

*An appreciation of the learning and ways of knowing that children
bring with them to school*

Again, it is in the programmes of study for Key Stage 1 that the need to
build on the child's abilities and experiences brought from home is
stressed. The case for continuing partnership with the home is also made.
It is a pity that this theme does not remain explicit throughout the programmes for the later stages.

A move of concern from teaching methods to learning strategies

The earlier part of the programmes of study are somewhat ambivalent on
this point, but in the later stages the emphasis is quite clearly on teaching
and there does appear to be a discontinuity in the programmes of study in
this respect.

*An awareness of the increasingly complex literacy demands of
modern technological society*

This is indicated explicitly in the statements of attainment at levels 1 and 2
where reference is made to book and non-book sources for reading such as
labels and menus. The linking of reading with craftwork also makes it clear

from the beginning that reading is presented as an activity that allows one to get things done.

This is built upon in levels 3 and 4 where it is reinforced in the use of information sources using classification systems, catalogues and databases and the developing skills of inference, deduction and the use of previous reading experience.

Further extension of these approaches occurs in levels 5 and 6 where there is reference to the recognition of fact or opinion in non-literary and media texts and whether evidence or persuasion are used; awareness of how writer's choice of language can have an effect on a reader. While at level 7 this is extended to include recognition of features of presentation that are used to inform, to regulate, to reassure or to persuade; and in levels 9 and 10 there is concern with the selection, retrieval, evaluation and combination of material from a wide range of reference sources.

As far as the programmes of study are concerned, from the very earliest stages reading material should include computer printout and visual display and at the later stages pupils should be aware of how texts such as reference books, brochures and consumer reports are structured.

*A move of concern for the education of an élite to education
for all*

In the programmes of study reference is made to the need to make use of non-sighted methods of reading and those who may have to use signing rather than reading aloud. It is stated clearly that both boys and girls should experience a wide range of children's literature.

One would assume then that school age children would be working at the levels appropriate to them. It is a pity then that such information about level of working should be made available to those other than parents or teachers.

*Changing patterns of employment that mean that education may be
seen as continuous and lifelong*

This is not mentioned explicitly, but certainly the approaches recommended might well be continued beyond school. But one can't help wondering if the emphasis on placing pupils at various levels and stages may not undermine the confidence and motivation which have been evident in approaches such as those developed in adult basic skills work which have greater emphasis on self-assessment.

Changing expectations of children, parents, community and central government

English in the National Curriculum No. 2 (1990) makes the expectations of central government explicit. The extent to which these mirror, or in the future mould the expectations of teachers, children, parents and community we shall have to wait to see. At present the document does not reflect our diverse multicultural, multiethnic and multilingual society.

Summary

The theoretical framework and practical strategies presented in this book appear to be consonant with the national curriculum documents in Scotland, England and Wales. Indeed, they may be used to identify weaknesses in them.

The rationale of the Scottish document does seem to be particularly close to the views presented in the earlier chapters, viewing language as communication and accepting the importance of the social and cultural context for its development. In the programmes of study the strands on 'awareness of genre' and 'knowledge about language' are similar to the approaches presented in Chapter 3 of this volume; while the strategies presented in Chapter 4 are close to those strands dealing with 'close reading', 'reading aloud', 'reading for information', 'reading for enjoyment' and 'finding and handling information'. The resource implications of the report, in terms of staff development relates directly to Chapter 6.

The English and Welsh document was analysed and found to relate in part to the changes listed in Chapter 1 of this volume. There is reference to group work; the importance of building on the child's knowledge is stressed at the early stages; and the expectations of central government are made explicit. Throughout the emphasis is on the use of a very wide range of whole texts of increasing complexity; reading activities are linked closely to the needs and demands of the real world, except that it is seemingly a monocultural and monolingual world; and it addresses the complex literacy demands of modern technological society. It is stronger on technology than on social and cultural context; at the later stages the emphasis is on teaching rather than on learning; and throughout there might have been greater emphasis on self-assessment in order to support flexible and continuous, lifelong education.

CHAPTER 6

The challenge for teacher education

What has been provided is a theoretical framework which summarizes the state of the art in our knowledge of children, language and learning. As such it should be relevant to all aspects of teacher education. In as much as language is central to learning both for the student and for the teacher the focus of this book can also be justified in this respect. However, the narrower focus is on reading development and this too can be seen as central to teacher education in terms of the reading development of the student and the teacher.

If we are serious about education being lifelong then the professional education and development of teachers must also be lifelong. Not only are the analysis and assimilation of current documents an essential part of the professional preparation and development of teachers, but so is instruction in the preparation and writing of reports related to these and strategies for reading them. Strategies recommended in this book for use with pupils may also be applied to the study of official curriculum documents and reports. They provide interesting materials for group reading and discussion activities involving prediction, sequencing and text marking.

In addition, the relationship of the content of this book to the requirements of the national curriculum documents ensures its relevance to teacher education.

In-service education

No matter how useful such approaches, they will be of no value if teachers themselves do not have the knowledge of language required to implement them. The argument of this section is that teachers can understand and apply such concepts without an academic background in linguistics and without following a lengthy course.

An example of a short course and its evaluation

An example of a short course, related to the notion of cohesion, and the evaluation of the course will be presented.

An immediate evaluation of a course for teachers gives no indication of the long-term effects on classroom practice. It is suggested that as little as three one-hour workshop sessions would be sufficient to raise the awareness of a group of educationists to the nature of cohesion in texts, and to have some influence on their practice three years after the course. I am indebted to the course member who suggested that it would be useful to find out what use had been made of the workshop content by other members of the course.

A questionnaire (Appendix 3) was prepared and sent to the twenty-two people who had expressed an interest in three cohesion one-hour workshops (Appendix 4) on their registration forms for a conference about reading. Not all of them necessarily attended the workshops. Nevertheless, 14 (over 60 per cent) of them completed and returned the questionnaire that was sent to them exactly three years after the course.
Of the 14 respondents:

- Two attended one workshop session.
- Five attended two workshop sessions.
- Six attended three workshop sessions.
- One did not respond to that question.

At the time of the workshops:

- Two were teachers of 4–8 year olds.
- One taught 4–13 year olds.
- Two taught 8–13 year olds.
- One taught 13+ year olds.
- Three were lecturers.
- Two were advisers or advisory teachers.
- Two were publishers.
- One was a former teacher working in a community home.

Since the conference 6 have changed their occupation:

- One teacher of 4–8 year olds worked as an advisory teacher for one year.
- The teacher of 4–13 year olds is now a part-time lecturer and researcher.
- The two teachers of 8–13 year olds are now deputy headteachers.
- The teacher of 13 year olds is now a part-time supply teacher.
- The former teacher working in a community home is now an education officer in a museum.

Of the fourteen respondents, all but one had heard of the notion of cohesion before attending the workshops. The majority of them (seven) had heard of cohesion through their reading; four had heard about it in lectures; one had been to a workshop; six had heard of it in other ways such as communication with others, from own use of written language, through UKRA, in the OU Reading Diploma Course, and in discussions.

All respondents felt that they knew more about cohesion at the end of the workshops than they did at the beginning.

At the end of the workshops, according to the respondents:

- Three were confident about identifying cohesive ties.
- Six were confident about identifying most ties.
- Five could identify some ties.

However, at the time of completing the questionnaires over three years later:

- Four felt confident about identifying cohesive ties.
- Three felt confident about identifying most cohesive ties in a text.
- Four could identify some ties in a text.
- One could identify a few ties.
- Two certainly could not identify cohesive ties from the five categories.

So over the three years a certain amount of polarization occurred, with some gaining confidence in identifying ties and others losing some skill in this area. This varied with perceptions of the usefulness of the activity and opportunities to put the knowledge into practice.

Ten of the respondents felt able to compare texts in terms of cohesive patterning; three did not; one did not respond to that question. However, the *yes/no* alternative responses were supplemented by comments written in by some of the respondents:

- to some extent;
- but not fully;
- just!
  involved in new research in this area.

These comments applied only to the *yes* category; it was clearly too wide. When asked whether they thought that the work on cohesion had any implications for their own practice:

- Eleven considered that it did.
- One thought that there probably were.
- One thought that there were possibly, but doubted it.
- One thought that there were none.

Since the workshops:

- Two have made regular use of insights from the workshops.
- Six have used aspects of the work from time to time.
- Two have used aspects of the work on the odd occasion.
- One has hardly ever used aspects of the work.
- Three have made no use at all of aspects of the work.

Nine responded to the question about how they had used insights from the workshops:

- Eight found it useful in understanding how texts work.
- Seven found it useful in identifying difficulties and ambiguities in texts.
- Five found it useful in understanding the reading process.
- Five found it useful in preparing materials for pupils.
- Five found it useful in communicating with teachers or students.
- Five found it useful in group reading activities.
- Two found it useful in helping children with their writing.
- Two found it useful in research or investigations.
- One found it useful in hearing children read.

The use made of insights would seem to be related to the age of the children taught and the occupation of the respondents.

Since the conference nine have gone on to find out more about cohesion, while five have not. Of these nine:

- Eight have done so through reading.
- Three from lectures.
- Three from workshops.
- The 'other' category consisted of:
  - (a) three discussion,
  - (b) one in use,
  - (c) one written articles and arranged a focus issue of a journal on cohesion,
  - (d) one carrying out research.

When asked if they thought they had gained anything from the workshops, even if they had made no practical use of the material: 11 said yes, three did not respond.

Eight of the group responded to the open-ended section that invited them to make any comments or provide further details that might be of interest. These are presented below.

One indicated that she had had little opportunity to make use of cohesion concepts working as a part-time temporary supply teacher:

> I do think that it made things clear for me from the beginning – I would always have been less sure of myself if I had learnt about it just from books.

In my work as a teacher of young children I was pleased that the cohesion work alerted me to aspects of texts, particularly reading schemes. This had two main implications for my work:

(i)   reference back either not clear or so far removed that it was very difficult for a halting reader to keep in mind;
(ii) simplified texts often contain so much ellipsis that they are not at all simple but are very difficult.

For the past year I have been working with an In-set Advisory Team in primary and secondary schools and found aspects of the work that looked at subject texts most helpful. For instance, I used cloze (deleting conjunctions and reference) as a group reading activity. I also formulated a 'model' for making sense of a science text.

In editing and writing one is continually aware of the factors that make for cohesion or fragmentation in written language. It is important to know when to choose either factor. I think the workshop helped by sharpening this awareness. I continue to benefit from it in editing at all levels.

During the workshops I mentioned that I thought encouraging children to make some kind of image or symbol on paper to stand for characters or events, perhaps on a file card, would be useful in comprehending the cohesive ties of reference. The children would hold up the appropriate image when asked about ties such as pronouns. I still think that something like this – a reference outside of language – is necessary for children having comprehension problems and helpful for others.

I would have liked to have followed up a case of a child prevented from becoming a competent reader because cohesion was not appreciated, then helped to better reading because cohesion had been absorbed. I was not convinced that cohesion is a factor in reading difficulties.

At the time of the conference I was an ex-teacher working for social services in a residential community home for adolescents, therefore my immediate use for cohesion work was very limited indeed. Since then I have re-entered the world of education and will be working closely with teachers and children as Education Officer at a museum. This will involve preparation of learning materials for a variety of age groups and interest and ability levels and an awareness of cohesive elements should be helpful.

I've used some of the ideas in one or two workshops for teachers that I've done, providing passages to look for collocation chains, and to point out cohesive ties used in sequencing a text etc., as well as with children sometimes. I did find it a stimulating workshop.

It would seem then from the response, over 60 per cent to a postal questionnaire, after a period of three years, that the group consisted of highly motivated and interested professionals.

All found something of interest in the workshops, although not all found it useful. The extent to which they have made any practical use of the concepts introduced would seem to be related to their own perceptions of the usefulness of the notions presented and their opportunity to work with children in classrooms on a regular basis.

Two further points would seem to emerge. It is not necessary to have a background in linguistics to come to terms with these concepts, nor does it seem to be necessary to have a lengthy course as long as there is support through further reading or discussion with interested colleagues.

This particular course lasted a total of three hours, but a short one-hour session could be incorporated into a staff Planned Activity Time concerned perhaps with the preparation of materials for thematic work.

One of the common pitfalls in materials prepared for young children or children with reading difficulties is the tendency to use pronouns to excess because they are short and easy to read aloud, though their overuse can lead to confusion as to who is doing what to whom! During the course just described it was discovered that in a very simple information text intended for young children the word 'it' occurred four times in a ten-word sentence. When this is combined with unfamiliar vocabulary such as 'bind' in the previous sentence then there may be problems:

> Then *it* bites *it* with *its* fangs and poisons *it*.

Two more recent examples that presented problems for her class are provided by Jennifer Eden (1991):

> In 1231, Eleanor, the daughter of King John, received permission from her brother, Henry III, to live in the castle. In 1233, however, *he* ordered it to be destroyed.

The children asked 'Who is *he*?'

> In 1190, John Marshall was allowed to live *there* for 'service of half a knight's fee'. [The word 'castle' had appeared in a previous sentence.]

The children asked where *there* was.

Further starting points are suggested in the final chapter of this book.

Initial teacher education

There are severe constraints of time and content laid down by national requirements for teacher education courses, but the relevance to national curricula justifies the inclusion of such topics. The difficult question is how it is to be done. The answer is that the approach must be twofold; it must be related to school based work and it must be embedded in activities and content across curriculum areas. It can be introduced through the prediction of difficulties in texts from different subject areas in terms of use of pronouns, substitutes or connectives. The following checklist of points to observe in preparing worksheets has also proved a useful introduction to the area:

1. If 'he', 'she', 'it', etc. are used is it quite clear what they are referring to?
2. If 'this', 'that', 'there', etc. are used is it quite clear what they are referring to?
3. If comparatives are being used, is it quite clear what is being compared?
4. If 'one', 'so', 'not', 'do' are used is it quite clear what they are substitutes for?
5. If sequences are dealt with, e.g. time, cause, contrast, is this implicit or would an 'and', 'so', 'but', or 'then' type of conjunction make it clearer?
6. If synonyms or antonyms are used would the likely readers recognize them as such either from their previous knowledge or from the text itself?

Students can prepare material, or choose a text for use in school, then identify possible areas of confusion, using the checklist. The original text should be used in school but checks on understanding of the sections predicted to cause difficulty should be made. Subsequently the findings may be shared, pooled and new guidelines drawn up in a workshop session.

School-based work on cultural diversity and the effects of text structure might be approached through the use of strategies adapted from Steffensen's study of reading comprehension across cultures (1981). For example, passages from different cultural settings may be prepared in the following manner. The passage is presented in a booklet so that on each page one more clause is exposed than on the preceding page, with all the remaining clauses blanked out. Pupils then read the text a clause at a time and are asked to describe what they have learned from the text and what they anticipate will follow. This is a complex area and students would have to work with individual children, but it is well worthwhile if it raises the student's awareness of the cultural assumptions made in texts presented to children in school. For full benefit the results would have to be pooled in a workshop or seminar session.

All of the activities recommended for children can be incorporated in the students' planning for school-based work.

Unfortunately, few institutions can offer a major subject study in Language, such as that in the Anglia Polytechnic BEd course, but there is a clearly identifiable need for the study of written discourse across the curriculum, in all teacher education courses.

Summary

It has been argued that the theoretical framework and practical strategies presented in this book are relevant to the initial and continuing professional education of teachers, both in terms of their practice and their own reading development. The implementation of national curricula documents merely strengthens the argument.

It has also been argued that such notions may be introduced to teachers without a lengthy course of language study. An example of such a course, and its evaluation were presented.

The constraints of time and content, laid down by central government, on initial teacher education courses was acknowledged. Nevertheless, it was stated that the theoretical framework and practical strategies outlined in the book could be introduced if they were related to school-based work and embedded in activities and content across curriculum areas.

CHAPTER 7

Communicating with colleagues, community, parents and other professionals

The development of a school policy on reading

In the light of the previous discussion it is suggested that the following questions might form part of a starter paper for staff discussion when developing or reviewing a school policy on reading. The questions derive directly from the points summarized at the end of Chapter 1. The first task would be to decide which, if any, of the questions are worth asking in your particular school.

1. How are texts used for reading chosen?
2. How are the culture and language traditions of the home and community shown to be respected and valued?
3. How is the difficulty of the texts assessed?
4. How do texts in use in other curriculum areas support the work of reading development?
5. What criteria are used in monitoring progression in the texts used and produced?
6. How can the use of complete and continuous texts be supported and developed throughout the school? Do the texts have to be read *by* the children or may they be read *to* them on occasion?
7. How can opportunities be provided for sustained reading of continuous texts?
8. How is group reading used? Could it be extended? Are group reading activities seen as opportunities for problem solving and tackling?

9. Is paired reading used? Could its use be extended including across curriculum areas?
10. How do you find out children's knowledge of and expectations about written language on their entry to school?
11. How do you find out the parents'/school board's/governors' expectations about reading development?
12. Are the contexts created for reading and writing comfortable, reassuring and naturalistic. Do they encourage confidence, motivation and learning?
13. Have you identified the learning strategies which you wish to encourage so that there can be consolidation across a wide range of resources and curriculum areas?
14. How is information technology used to extend, support and enhance literacy development?
15. How do you extend and support the quality of literacy experience and competence of all the children?
16. Are children encouraged to question texts? How do you encourage the confidence and attitudes to written language that welcome problem tackling, problem solving and change as a challenge?
17. How can field trips, visits and links with industry be exploited to support reading development?
18. How confident do you feel about explaining the school reading policy to your colleagues, to a student, to the children, to parents, to your school board/governors, to the local press, to community groups, to other professionals, to local industrialists, to elected representatives on councils? What kind of support would help you to become more confident?

It is quite clear that the school policy on reading development should be the basis for discussion with parents and with other professionals. A major role of policy development should be as a clarification and consolidation exercise that enables the core principles to be exposed, so that even the newest member of staff is both confident and enthusiastic about articulating them. Such confidence comes from a sense of ownership, from arguing, from justifying and from caring about the quality of learning and teaching that occurs in your own school.

Primary/secondary liaison in reading

How can continuity in reading development be supported across the primary secondary divide?

To address the bad news first, a major problem is that reading does not appear as a subject on the secondary school timetable. Whether or not this is a problem may depend on the secondary school's policies on learning support and on language across the curriculum as well as the extent to which these policies are realized within subject departments. At least primary schools can acknowledge the very real constraints of secondary school timetabling, the demands of public examinations and the organizational demands of dealing with large numbers of staff and pupils. On the other hand, secondary staff can acknowledge the professional expertise of primary colleagues.

The good news is that the national curricula bridge the gap between primary and secondary education and thus provide a framework for discussion. Whether the resources will be available to capitalize on this unique opportunity is beyond the remit of this book, but the potential certainly exists.

The curriculum and assessment changes in secondary education which have occurred throughout the United Kingdom have directed attention to the assessment of reading at that level. One study which addresses the issues in a thorough and practical manner, starting with the realities of the classroom is Fyfe and Mitchell's *Reading Strategies and Their Assessment* (1985). One of the topics in that volume could well serve as a starting point for discussion separately within school staffs and then in combined primary secondary groups. The topics include:

- Using telephone directories.
- Using a dictionary.
- Reading directions.
- Filling in a form.
- Novel reading.
- Reading a short story.

Alternatively, Eden's (1991) brief paper, which focuses on the development of reading for information in a middle school (9–13 year olds), might be used as a starter paper for discussion.

Another approach which might be valuable would be for primary and secondary staffs to look together at some of the materials and approaches used in adult basic skills work, so that there is a wider perspective and greater coherence and progression in the approaches and resources used.

So much excellent work of this type has been done but it is not always as widely accessible as it should be, and valuable teacher time is spent in replicating existing work. It is much more profitable for time to be spent in adapting and adjusting materials and approaches to the needs of individual or groups of schools.

What then are the questions which should be discussed in primary secondary dialogue? I would suggest that the following are worth considering:

1. How are non-readers taught to read when they come to school? This should be covered briefly and succinctly drawing on primary school policy documents and booklets.
2. How is reading supported throughout the primary school for all children?
3. What are the reading demands across the curriculum areas in the first two years of secondary education?
4. What are the organizational problems faced by secondary staffs in supporting reading development in the first two years of secondary education?
5. Can mixed groups of primary secondary teachers suggest positive strategies which may be used at primary and secondary level to help to overcome these difficulties?
6. What are the reading demands made by public examinations across the curriculum areas?
7. What are the organizational problems faced when attempting to support reading development in the later years of secondary schooling?
8. What are the reading requirements of vocational courses and in work placements in secondary and further education?
9. How are these approached?
10. Are there overlaps or approaches which may be exploited across the age ranges?
11. What specialist knowledge of the language characteristics of their curriculum areas do secondary teachers have to pass on to their colleagues?
12. What experience of organization, of resources and of the integration of curriculum areas do primary teachers have to pass on to their colleagues?

These are only a beginning, but making a start is always the most difficult part.

What does the community see of literacy development in your school? (Figures 5–8)

As publicists, on the whole, educationists are dismal failures. By training we are encouraged to focus on what can be improved. We are often so busy doing so that we do not share what we are doing well with the wider community. Then we are surprised by unfair and uninformed criticism in the media. Even when we are aware of this, there is still no more time to do anything about it, and it is only recently that education authorities have recognized their responsibility for supporting teachers in this respect.

Figure 5   We like this story

Figure 6   We can share it with our parents if we act it

Figure 7   The bigger girls will be narrators

Figure 8   They like making their favourite stories into plays as well

However, what we can do is to consider the instances in which we are observed by the community and consider how they may be used to inform the public of the value accorded literacy development in our schools and the quality of the children's educational experiences. These instances may be divided into three groups namely, visits out of school, visitors to school and activities within school that are open to the general public.

What are the literacy activities that are normally linked with visits out of school? We are used to seeing children with clipboards and worksheets, with tape recorders, with cameras, with materials for drawing, collecting and measuring. Notes are made during the visit and thank you letters are written, but do we share with the people visited the work that results from the visit?

One of our school's most successful links was with the Forestry Commission when a visit to observe processes in forestry management was followed up a term later by a visit from one of the foresters to talk about landscape policy. This visit enabled him to see some of the children's work and at a later date he was sent a copy of the school newspaper account of his talk.

Do we take reference books with us when we go on visits? Are the people we visit aware of the children's research skills and their ability to use reference material? Sometimes the children's information is more accurate than that of the adults involved. Not every guide to historic buildings has read the most recent edition of the guidebook, we discovered.

In our links with industry and our visits out of school do we try to find out the reading and writing demands of the jobs we observe? What are the purposes for which reading is required in that particular task?

The advantage of visitors to the school from the community is that they can see reading activities in action in the school. However, reading is, on the whole, a silent and solitary activity so that displays of school work may have to be labelled to make the reading aspects of the work explicit. This is usually done extremely well as far as book studies are concerned but do we ever consider listing information books and other reference material used in producing displays or models?

Do our libraries reflect our view of literacy development? What messages do visitors to the school receive from it? Excellent suggestions for improving school/class library use and appearance are provided by Gawith (1987) in *Library Alive*.

Corridors and cloakroom areas are often used to display photographs of school activities. On the whole these tend to be more active and colourful activities. Might there be a place for a display of photographs of different types of reading and related activities? Might there be photographs and texts that illustrate development and progression in reading across the primary school age range?

The hope is that visitors will then relate what they have seen to a wider audience in the community. Recently a local naturalist brought a young barn owl to visit us in school. Yes, *The Owl Who Was Afraid of the Dark* is one of our favourite books and even the youngest child in the school can read the chapter headings, since they form part of a classroom display. So we were very thrilled and honoured to have such a visitor. We were also delighted when our thank you letter to the naturalist appeared in the next edition of the magazine of the local natural history society.

Another occasion when visitors come to school is when there is some kind of performance or sharing of work in the form of an assembly, or an end of term concert. This provides one of the few opportunities for reading aloud with a clear purpose. This can also involve the children in the extremely useful task of adapting a favourite story that has been read, to a form that is suitable for entertainment and for a larger audience. In tackling this problem children also become aware of some of the genre differences between narrative and drama.

What do parents see of literacy development in your school?

Some of the issues under this heading have been dealt with already. Points have been made about the role of the school policy document and the school booklet in clarifying communication with parents. All of the points regarding visitors to the school apply equally to parents. Perhaps one area that has been neglected is the area where children read aloud to other children. Pre-school children are thrilled on their visits to school if they are read to by older children. I recall one young friend of mine at playgroup telling his friends that Duncan (age seven) was coming to stay and bragging that 'Duncan can read books'. A great deal of practical advice on involving parents, and others in shared reading projects in schools is provided in a companion volume in this series *Shared Reading in Practice* (Davis and Stubbs 1988). And Campbell (1991) provides a useful analysis of interaction while hearing children read.

Further points to consider, however, are whether parents are aware of the extent of liaison between primary and secondary schools and ways in which they can help to support the young person at the time of transition. Are they aware of the genre differences (Littlefair 1991) which their children will be faced with in the secondary school? How do they see the primary school literacy policy relating to secondary school expectations, values and demands; or to the values and demands of the wider community?

Equally, to what extent does literacy figure in our pre-school liaison? How could we support and extend what is already going on at home? In the discussions about increasing the number of nursery-school or class places very little is said of the support which such provision may give to parents, in terms of the strength of informal links which allow parents to discuss very real concerns which might seem trivial in a more formal setting, or when the teacher seems to be surrounded by hordes of children. Such occasions, very often over a kettle while making tea or coffee, can ease concerns considerably, and in at least one case I can remember, lead to literacy development work with the parent concerned. The task is very much more difficult in primary schools.

Communicating with other professionals

Do we ever consider seriously the need to communicate curriculum matters to the other professionals with whom we are involved? This is easiest with those groups whose training overlaps with teaching such as educational psychologists or speech therapists, but even here there are pitfalls and variations in training, some of which may have stressed medical rather than educational perspectives. Suffice it to say that we need not assume that every professional involved with children in our school necessarily understands our school policy on reading. In some cases it may be appropriate to offer a copy of the school booklet.

Conclusion

The focus of this book on reading may seem rather narrow in curricular terms. However, if one views reading as a form of communication, and accepts the importance of the social and cultural setting in any human interaction then very much wider issues such as those addressed in this chapter must be considered. In terms of the model of reading presented in this book one must consider the reader, the writer and the text and the relationship between them in their social and cultural context. In doing so we should not neglect the complexities of written language nor as Bruner (1982) has pointed out, forget to give credit, to the child who learns to read, for the task achieved.

Summary

A starter paper for staff discussion on school reading policy development or review was presented. The questions in the paper were based on points raised in Chapter 1. The role of a policy document in crystallizing communication with parents and other professionals was also discussed.

Questions and approaches to literacy development and continuity in education, related to primary/secondary liaison were presented. Issues related to community and parental perceptions of literacy development and communication with other professionals were discussed and some practical points noted.

Finally, the links between the model of reading presented in this book and the content of this chapter were made.

CHAPTER 8

Epilogue

The changes that have occurred in our view of reading over the past 40 years have done so at a time when the complexity of human activity is recognized by psychologists, linguists, sociologists and educationists. The time of simple answers to simple questions is over for theorists, and practitioners require insights that acknowledge the social, emotional, linguistic and cultural interaction of learning and teaching in a fast-changing world.

The changes have been summarized in Chapter 1 and a focus for practical implications for teaching and learning has been drawn up. Since reading is viewed as communication, and as such, like any other form of human interaction, the social and cultural context are of prime importance, then the focus for practice is much wider than one might have assumed from a concern with only reading, it includes concern with such general issues as policy, progression and parental, community and governmental expectations.

It has been argued, in this volume, that an interactive model of reading, involving the flexible use of all the cue systems – phonic, grammatical, meaning, previous knowledge of texts and of the world – placed within a systemic functional view of language may provide such insights as those required by practitioners; relating as it does, to reader, writer and text. It accommodates the major points raised in Chapters 1 and 2. It takes account of reading as involving both language and thought. It permits the social and cultural setting of reader, text and writer to be considered. It is clearly concerned with language at the discourse level, as language in use and as communication. It is of a form that is easily translated into classroom terms while retaining sufficient linguistic detail to permit it to be used to diagnose strengths and weaknesses in writers, readers and texts. It has been employed successfully in such complex areas as the cross-cultural study of comprehension (Steffensen 1981).

It is this linking of all three that gives the notion such power and such validity for the classroom. Such an approach has been criticized and misunderstood for being too text based or even word based. However, it has been argued here that this is not the case and that any robust model of comprehension must accommodate reader, writer and text. It must also take account of the patterning of text beyond the sentence. Weaknesses in practice in the past have been identified as the lack of development in reading beyond the early stages and the scant attention paid to the development of reading of non-narrative texts.

Evidence has been presented here and elsewhere (Chapman 1987, E. Anderson 1990) that with increasing age and experience of using texts, children appear to develop awareness of the vertical patterning of texts. This ability would seem to develop alongside reading comprehension and with progress in school work. Children's awareness of the linguistic structure of texts can be developed. Teachers and students with little or no linguistic training can find it a fascinating way into the study of texts, particularly when it involves school based work across the curriculum.

The implications for teaching are consonant with the recommendations of the Kingman Report (DES 1988) and the national curricula documents on language. All of these call for teachers to be knowledgeable about the structure of English. Within this, cohesion is an important notion. It has a valuable contribution to make to the teacher's concept of the reading process, providing a bridge between the syntactic and semantic cue systems of a psycholinguistic model of reading; or between the intermediate and comprehension skills in a skills model; though it is probably more usefully perceived as part of the textual function of language linking to the interpersonal and ideational functions and allowing interaction in either direction in an interactive model. In simple terms the text, content, writer and reader are linked together and interact. They interact through the text and the fluent and experienced reader uses a range of strategies that are appropriate to the text and the purpose for reading.

It has been argued that a knowledge of such patterning allows teachers to anticipate and predict difficulties that pupils may experience in texts. And a list for checking teacher-made and other materials was presented in Chapter 6. A knowledge of features of texts can also assist teacher–child interaction and teacher intervention in a number of settings. It can provide insight into the differences between spoken and written language for the teacher and child working on early literacy development using a language experience approach. The insights with regard to teacher-constructed materials can also be used in conferencing concerned with the redrafting of a pupil's writing. Similarly, in hearing a child read it can raise the teacher's awareness of possible ambiguities and misunderstandings. Likewise it can assist in the formulation of questions to check understanding of what has been read. Such questions, though usually of a simple wh- type, therefore not more difficult to read than the passage, nevertheless tend to involve textually implicit comprehension.

It is probably at its most powerful in directed group reading and thinking activities where deletions from cohesive chains may direct attention across sentence boundaries. Replacing deleted connectives is a particularly worthwhile activity. In group sequencing an awareness of the patterning of texts assists the teacher in identifying the types of cues that are or are not being used. In group prediction activities a knowledge of cohesion allows the teacher to monitor how individual awareness of the content domain of a passage develops. It is also a useful teaching technique to draw children's attention to the writer's use or abuse of cohesive chains.

The changes outlined in Chapter 1 and the model presented in Chapter 2 raise important questions about classroom practice and emphasize the need for schools to communicate more effectively with the wider community. It is hoped that this book will help teachers to understand some of the thinking behind the increasing demands being made on them and in turn assist them in the clearer and more confident articulation of their policies.

Summary

1. The need to consider reading as communication was identified.
2. An interactive model of reading, involving the flexible use of all cue systems was presented.
3. Placed within a Hallidayan view of language it allows account to be taken of the social and cultural context of the reader, the writer and the text.
4. Included in this model is the notion of cohesion which focuses on the text but allows access to the content and to the social and cultural context.
5. Weaknesses in practice in the past were identified as lack of attention to development beyond the early stages and little support in the use of non-narrative texts.
6. The relationship between awareness of cohesive chains and comprehension was discussed.
7. Developing readers have increasing awareness of the linguistic patterning of text. This appears to be linked to the use of larger units of language across sentence boundaries.
8. Evidence was reviewed that indicates that linguistic features apparently understood in spoken language are not necessarily understood in written texts in a range of registers.

9. The theoretical model presented in this book can be applied in the classroom and in courses for teachers.

10. It was argued that reading development must take account of complete and complex texts; the power of discussion; the importance of interaction; the use of a wider range of materials and settings for reading; and the expectations of the wider community.

11. Neither model nor strategies conflict with national curricula requirements. In some cases they may enhance them. They lend themselves to use in teacher education courses related to the national curricula requirements in reading.

12. The changes of the past 40 years have made increasing demands on teachers to co-operate and communicate with the wider community. It is hoped that this book may help them in articulating their policies with greater confidence and clarity.

A summary of cohesive ties

In order to avoid the common pitfall of looking at Halliday and Hasan's notion in isolation for their overall view of language it is particularly useful to clarify two concepts before considering Halliday and Hasan's notion of cohesion. The first is a concept of particular concern to those interested in the development of literacy and reading fluency, that is the predictability of texts; and the second is Halliday's concept of text. The starting point for an understanding of the predictability of text for Halliday begins with the social context; consonant with his view of language as a social semiotic he states that:

> A social context is a semiotic structure which we may interpret in terms of three variables: a 'field' of social process (what is going on), a 'tenor' of social relationships (who are taking part) and a 'mode' of symbolic interaction (how meanings are exchanged) . . . The linguistic system, in other words, is organized in such a way that the social context is predictive of the text. (1978: 189)

To summarize:

> The categories of field, tenor and mode are thus determinants and not components of speaking; collectively they serve to predict text. (1978: 62)

Such a view of the predictability of texts would appear to be close to that of the schemata theorists with a top-down perspective on reading. However, to understand Halliday and Hasan's concept of cohesion, which they view as part of the textual function of language, it is also necessary to understand their notion of text. Perhaps the clearest account appears in Halliday (1978: 109):

> In other words, a text is a semantic unit; it is the basic unit of the semantic process.
>   At the same time, text represents choice. A text is 'what is meant', selected from the total set of options that constitute what can be meant. In other words, text can be defined as actualized meaning potential.

Indeed, Halliday (1985) claims that it is the textual metafunctional component of meaning in language that 'breathes relevance' into the other two components of meaning the ideational or reflective and the interpersonal or active.

Most studies relating cohesion and reading have taken as their starting point the concept of cohesion as presented in *Cohesion in English* (Halliday and Hasan 1976). That would seem to be a practice worth following, at least as an introduction.

Halliday and Hasan view cohesion as a principal resource for text construction. In the preface to *Cohesion in English* they introduce it thus:

Cohesive relations are relations between two or more elements in a text that are independent of the structure; for example between a personal pronoun and an antecedent proper name, such as *John . . . he.* A semantic relation of this kind may be set up either within a sentence or between sentences; with the consequence that, when it crosses a sentence boundary it has the effect of making the two sentences cohere with one another. (1976: vii)

As already indicated, Halliday and Hasan see cohesion as a relational concept:

. . . It is not the presence of a particular class of item that is cohesive, but the relation between one item and another. (1976: 12)

This relationship between one item and another they call a cohesive tie. Indeed, in texts of any length chains of cohesive ties occur and it is with these chains that Halliday and Hasan are concerned in their later work.

The categories of cohesive ties presented by Halliday and Hasan in 1976 were those of reference, substitution, ellipsis, conjunction and lexical cohesion.

Halliday and Hasan use the term reference to describe those items in the language that instead of being interpreted semantically in their own right, make reference to something for their interpretation. Halliday and Hasan state that in English these items are personal, demonstrative and comparative, e.g.

(a) *Personal* – *Plato* was a Greek philosopher, born in 427 BC. *His* idea was called *The Republic.*
(b) *Demonstrative* – In wet weather *you might get stuck*. Men working on a building site have *this* problem, so they build their simple railway.
(c) *Comparative* – From the Masters and from ancient lore-books Ged learned what he could about such beings as this *shadow* he had loosed: little was there to learn. No *such* creature was described or spoken of directly.

(a) Contains an example of personal reference, the cohesive tie being the relationship between *Plato* and *His*.

(b) The tie between *you might get stuck* and *this* is an example of a demonstrative relationship.
(c) The tie between *shadow* and *such* signals a comparative relationship.

As Halliday and Hasan point out, reference is a semantic relation, but substitution is more of a grammatical relation, in as much as the substitute as a general rule, is of the same grammatical class as the item for which it substitutes. The criterion for classification is the grammatical function of the substitute, and in English the three possible types of substitution are nominal, verbal and clausal. In the following examples:

(a) *Nominal* – Some car *parts* wear out. New *ones* must be fitted.
(b) *Verbal* – All the animals in this book *feed their young with milk*. Animals which *do this* are mammals.
(c) *Clausal* – I said, 'Yeah, that's right', and he said, 'Well, now *you'll be signing full pro*'.
'I hope *so*', I said, though I must admit it encouraged me, hearing Mike say that, because normally he didn't give anything away, old Mike.

The relationship between *parts* and *ones* is a nominal substitute cohesive tie; while in (b) the relationship between *feed their young with milk* and *do this* is a verbal substitution; and in (c) the relationship between *you'll be signing full pro* and *so* is a clausal substitution.

Similarly, Halliday and Hasan (1976: 143) state that:

> An elliptical item is one which, as it were, leaves specific structural slots to be filled from elsewhere. This is exactly the same as presupposition by substitution, except that in substitution an explicit 'counter' is used, e.g. *one* or *do*, as a place-marker for what is presupposed, whereas in ellipsis nothing is inserted in the slot. That is why we say that ellipsis can be regarded as substitution by zero.

Consequently, the sub-categories of ellipsis are the same as those for substitution, namely nominal, verbal and clausal. Examples of each one are presented below:

(a) *Nominal* – He next looked the pieces over very carefully. Some of them were no use at all, but some * were long and thin.
(b) *Verbal* – Rover set out to find if the gas turbine could *be adapted* to a motor car. It could * and it was * and in 1952, the Rover JET 1 set up the first officially recognized international speed records for turbine-powered cars.
(c) *Clausal* – Which oxide of carbon have you made? How did you tell * ?

(a), (b) and (c) are examples of nominal, verbal and clausal ellipsis respectively. In each case the second sentence cannot be fully understood without reference to the first sentence in the pair. In (a) the relationship is with a noun, in (b) with a verb and in (c) with a clause.

The fourth type of cohesive relation, conjunction, differs from those already mentioned, as Halliday and Hasan (1976: 227) make clear:

> With conjunction, on the other hand, we move into a different type of semantic relation, one which is no longer any kind of a search instruction, but a specification of the way in which what is to follow is systematically connected to what has gone before . . . in describing conjunction as a cohesive device, we are focusing attention not on the semantic relations as such, as realized throughout the grammar of the language, but on one particular aspect of them, namely the function they have of relating to each other linguistic elements that occur in succession but are not related by other, structural means.

Halliday and Hasan (1976) adopt a scheme of four sub-categories of conjunction, namely additive, adversative, causal and temporal. Examples of each are presented in (a), (b), (c) and (d) below:

(a) *Additive* – The stick grew into a skeleton. *And* before the farmer had started to give it flesh, Jan cried out, 'A canoe'.
(b) *Adversative* – Often a cheap microscope is shaped to look like an expensive one in a laboratory. *But* lenses are far more important than outward appearances.
(c) *Causal* – 'Damsel', answered Beaumains politely, 'you may say to me what you wish, but never will I turn back. *For* I have promised King Arthur to undertake your adventure – and achieve it I will, or die in the attempt'.
(d) *Temporal* – Once all the boxes are there they are opened, and the papers mixed together so that it is no longer possible to tell from which box they came. *Then* the count can begin.

(a) provides an example of additive conjunction through *And* between the two sentences. In (b) *But* signals an adversative connection between the two sentences. Similarly, in (c) *For* signals a causal relationship and in (d) *Then* makes a temporal relationship explicit.

The final group of cohesive relations identified by Halliday and Hasan is lexical cohesion. This is the cohesive effect achieved by the selection of vocabulary.

In Halliday and Hasan's classification there are two sub-groupings, namely reiteration and collocation. Reiteration is described as:

> a form of lexical cohesion which involves the repetition of a lexical item, at one end of the scale; the use of a general word to refer back to a lexical item, at the other end of the scale; and a number of things in between – the use of a synonym, near-synonym, or superordinate . . . All these instances have in common the fact that one lexical item refers back to another, to which it is related by having a common referent. (1976: 278)

Halliday and Hasan (1976) go on to state that collocation is the most problematic part of lexical cohesion. Martin (1981) discusses these problems and ways of overcoming them, but as an introduction, the following description will suffice:

> In general, any two lexical items have similar patterns of collocation – that is, tending to appear in similar contexts – will generate a cohesive force if they occur in adjacent sentences. (1976: 286)

Examples of reiteration and of collocation are presented in (a) and (b):

(a) *Reiteration* – It is also important that *milk* is put into clean bottles. Flies like drinking *milk*, and they carry disease.
(b) *Collocation* – Those with *gold* coins were to be the Rulers, called Guardians: those with *silver* ones were to make up the army, police and civil service, called Auxiliaries, and those with *iron* or *bronze* coins were to work providing food and other basic needs for the community.

In (a) *milk* is repeated in the second sentence. However, in (b) the collocation is provided by a chain of lexical items the metals *gold, silver, iron, bronze.*

Analysis of comprehension questions

Apple For The Teacher

Q.1   Previous knowledge
Q.2   Tie undeleted – personal reference
Q.3   Implicit connection – sentence order
Q.4   Tie deleted – substitute clausal   *so*
Q.5   Overall understanding of passage
Q.6   Tie undeleted – connective additive
Q.7   Implicit connection – sentence order
Q.8   Tie deleted – substitute verbal   *did*
Q.9   Previous knowledge
Q.10 Tie deleted – connective causal   *So*
Q.11 Overall understanding of the passage
Q.12 Tie deleted – connective temporal   *Next morning*

Snow Pictures

Q.1   Tie deleted – reference demonstrative   *the*
Q.2   Tie not deleted – reference personal
Q.3   Implicit connection – sentence order
Q.4   Tie deleted – connective temporal   *then*
Q.5   Tie not deleted – ellipsis
Q.6   Overall understanding of the passage
Q.7   Tie deleted – substitute nominal   *one*
Q.8   Tie not deleted – connective temporal
Q.9   Previous knowledge
Q.10 Implicit connection – sentence order
Q.11 Tie deleted – substitute verbal   *did it*

Q.12   Tie not deleted – reference demonstrative
Q.13   Overall understanding of the passage
Q.14   Previous knowledge

Wizard of Earthsea

Q.1   Deleted reference comparative   *such*
Q.2   General
Q.3   Undeleted reference comparative
Q.4   Deleted connective additive   *and*
Q.5   Implicit connection sentence order
Q.6   Undeleted connective temporal
Q.7   Deleted substitute verbal   *So did*
Q.8   General
Q.9   Undeleted lexical collocate
Q.10   Deleted lexical reiteration   *trees*
Q.11   Implicit connection sentence order
Q.12   Deleted reference personal   *him*
Q.13   Previous knowledge
Q.14   Previous knowledge

Sir Gareth

Q.1   Deleted connective causal   *For*
Q.2   Undeleted reference comparative
Q.3   General
Q.4   Deleted reference personal   *they*
Q.5   Undeleted lexical reiteration
Q.6   General
Q.7   Deleted connective adversative   *But*
Q.8   Undeleted lexical reiteration
Q.9   Implicit connection by sentence order
Q.10   Deleted substitute clausal   *so*
Q.11   Undeleted connective causal
Q.12   Implicit connection by sentence order
Q.13   Deleted lexical collocate   *slew*
Q.14   Undeleted connective causal
Q.15   Previous knowledge
Q.16   Deleted connective additive   *And*
Q.17   Undeleted connective adversative

Q.18   Previous knowledge
Q.19   Deleted reference comparative   *so*
Q.20   Undeleted connective additive
Q.21   Deleted connective causal   *Then*
Q.22   Deleted reference demonstrative   *this*
Q.23   Deleted reference comparative   *so*
Q.24   Deleted connective additive   *Moreover*

Royal Albert Bridge

Q.1   Deleted comparative reference   *Another*
Q.2   Implicit connection by sentence order
Q.3   Undeleted reference demonstrative
Q.4   Previous knowledge
Q.5   Deleted reference demonstrative   *This*
Q.6   General
Q.7   Deleted connective temporal   *First*
Q.8   General
Q.9   Deleted substitute verbal   *do this*
Q.10   Implicit connection by sentence order
Q.11   Undeleted temporal connective
Q.12   Deleted lexical reiteration   *girders*
Q.13   Previous knowledge
Q.14   Deleted lexical collocate   *road*

A Stuart Family in the Civil War

Q.1   General
Q.2   Undeleted comparative reference
Q.3   Implicit connection by sentence order
Q.4   Undeleted connective causal
Q.5   Previous knowledge
Q.6   Undeleted personal reference
Q.7   Previous knowledge
Q.8   Undeleted lexical collocate
Q.9   General
Q.10   Deleted lexical collocate   *forces*
Q.11   Implicit connection by sentence order
Q.12   Deleted lexical reiteration   *soldiers*
Q.13   Deleted clausal substitute   *so*

Microscopes

Q.1   Deleted connective adversative   *But*
Q.2   General
Q.3   Undeleted personal reference
Q.4   Deleted personal reference   *it*
Q.5   General
Q.6   Undeleted demonstrative reference
Q.7   Deleted nominal substitute
Q.8   Implicit connection by sentence order
Q.9   Deleted comparative reference   *more*
Q.10 Implicit connection by sentence order
Q.11 Deleted connective causal   *Therefore*
Q.12 Previous knowledge
Q.13 Deleted reference demonstrative   *the*
Q.14 Previous knowledge

Retrievers

Q.1   Previous knowledge
Q.2   Deleted reference personal   *they*
Q.3   Undeleted lexical reiteration
Q.4   Previous knowledge
Q.5   Deleted connective causal   *So*
Q.6   Undeleted lexical collocation
Q.7   Implicit connection by sentence order
Q.8   Deleted lexical collocate   *country*
Q.9   General
Q.10 General
Q.11 Implicit connection by sentence order

Questionnaire sent to workshop participants

According to records of the conference in Edinburgh you expressed an interest in the workshop sessions on 'Cohesive Elements and Suitability of Middle School Texts'.

I am interested, after three years, to find out if any aspects of the workshops have proved of use in your work, or indeed if you found it a complete waste of time. I realize that everyone involved in education is under great pressure at the present, but if you would be prepared to respond to the following questions I would be most grateful.

How many of the workshops did you attend?
Please circle the appropriate number.

    0   1   2   3

Were you at that time one or more of the following?

If you have changed occupation since 1981 please indicate below under number 12.

1. Teacher of 4–8 year olds
2. Teacher of 8–13 year olds
3. Teacher of 13+ year olds
4. Lecturer
5. Headteacher
6. Adviser or Advisory Teacher
7. Publisher
8. Writer
9. Researcher
10. Student
11. Other
12. Changed occupation since 1981 to ———

Had you heard of the notion of cohesion before attending the workshops?

1. No
2. Yes

If you answered Yes to the last question how had you heard of cohesion? Please indicate the source, if possible providing specific details alongside.	1. Reading 2. Lecture 3. Workshop 4. Other
Did you feel that you knew any more about cohesion at the end of the workshops than you did at the beginning?	1. No 2. Yes
Were you able to identify cohesive ties from the five main categories at the end of the workshops?	1. Certainly not 2. Could identify a few ties 3. Could identify some ties 4. Confident about identifying most ties in a text 5. Confident about identifying cohesive ties
Are you now able to identify cohesive ties from the five main categories?	1. Certainly not 2. Can identify a few ties 3. Can identify some ties 4. Confident about identifying most ties in a text 5. Confident about identifying cohesive ties
Do you feel able to compare texts in terms of cohesive patterning?	1. No 2. Yes
At the end of the workshops did you consider that there were any practical implications for your work?	1. No 2. Possibly, but doubt it 3. There might be 4. There probably are 5. Yes
Since the workshops have you made any use of any aspect of work presented in the workshops?	1. No 2. Hardly ever 3. On an odd occasion 4. From time to time 5. Regularly
If you have made any use of work presented in the workshops has it been . . .	1. in understanding the reading process 2. in understanding how texts work

3. in identifying difficulties and
   ambiguities in texts
4. in preparing materials for
   pupils
5. in helping children with their
   writing
6. in group reading activities
7. in hearing children read
8. in communicating with
   teachers or students
9. in research or investigations

Have you found out more about   1. No
cohesion since the conference?   2. Yes

If so, how?   1. Reading
Please specify.   2. Lecture
    3. Workshop
    4. Other

Even if you have made no practical   1. No
use of material from the workshops   2. Yes
do you think you gained anything
from them?

Please use this space for any comments you wish to make or for any further
details you think may be of interest.

If you would like a copy of the findings of this survey please indicate, and
one will be sent to you by the end of this year.

1. Yes
2. No

Thank you for your help,

Eleanor Anderson

Outline of three workshops on cohesion

Three workshops on the identification of cohesive ties in middle school texts

Heriot Watt University, Edinburgh, 27–31 July 1981.
It is assumed that the participants will be fairly knowledgeable about reading.

Aims

1. To introduce the concept of cohesion.
2. To enable participants to identify cohesive ties from the five main categories.
3. To enable participants to analyse and compare texts from different genres in terms of their cohesion.
4. To provide participants with an opportunity to consider the practical implications of the work carried out in the workshops for their practice in school.

Time

3 × 1 hour sessions

Materials

Overhead projector
Coloured pens
Copies of 'Summary of Cohesive Ties'

Copies of passages to be analysed
Texts to be brought by participants

Workshop 1

1. Working individually, place in order of difficulty three versions of a short story. Make notes justifying the order.
2. Working as a group, go through a cohesion analysis of one version of the story with the workshop leaders.
3. In pairs, work through a cohesion analysis of the other two versions of the story.
4. As a group, compare the analyses of the three versions of the story.
5. As a group consider the following questions:
   (i)   How would you order the passages now?
   (ii) Has the cohesion analysis suggested any changes in the order?
   (iii) Has working through the passages provided any new insights into the nature of texts?

Homework

1. Passages will be available for further practice in cohesion analysis.
2. If possible try out the three versions of the story with children. Which one do they think is the most difficult and why? If appropriate do a miscue analysis of their reading of the stories.

Workshop 2

1. Report back on homework.
2. In pairs, carry out a cohesion analysis of a fiction passage and a non-fiction passage dealing with the same topic.
3. As a group compare the analyses of the two passages in terms of number, type, distribution and chaining of the ties.
4. As a group suggest possible differences between the use of cohesion in fiction and in non-fiction texts.

Homework

Further texts will be available to continue the fiction/non-fiction comparison.

Bring own texts for the final workshop, to cover as wide a range of subjects as possible.

Workshop 3

1. Report back on differences between fiction and non-fiction texts analysed for homework.
2. Individually, analyse own texts brought to the workshop.
3. Compare analyses in pairs.
4. Report back to the group as a whole.
5. Consider as a group any differences that seem to be related to subject area.
6. Consider, as a group, whether the analyses carried out have:
   (i) any practical implications for work in school?
   (ii) provided any insights into characteristics of texts used in schools?

Postscript

What about teacher-prepared materials, tests and exam questions?

It may be possible to attempt to work on cohesive harmony if the group is particularly quick and hard working.

References

Anderson, E. (1979). *The Reading Behaviour of a Group of Children of Families of West Indian Origin*. Unpublished MPhil thesis, University of Nottingham, School of Education.

Anderson, E. (1983a). 'Cohesion in the classroom', *Australian Journal of Reading*, 6(1): 35–42.

Anderson, E. (1983b).'Reading and the bilingual child'. In N. Miller (ed.) *Bilingualism and Reading Disability*, London: Croom Helm, pp. 154–66.

Anderson, E. (1984a). 'Don't close the door on cloze'. In D. Dennis (ed.) *Reading: Meeting Children's Special Needs*, London: Heinemann Educational Books, pp. 177–80.

Anderson, E. (1984b). 'Kohaesion – og laereren'. In *Laesning Laese Rapport 11*, Dragor, Denmark: Danish Reading Association.

Anderson, E. (1988). 'Foreword' to C. Davis and R. Stubbs (eds) *Shared Reading in Practice*, Milton Keynes: Open University Press, pp. vii–ix.

Anderson, E. (1990). *The Implications of Recent Research on Cohesion for Teacher Education in Reading*. Unpublished PhD thesis, The Open University.

Anderson, J. (1976). *Psycholinguistic Experiments in Foreign Language Testing*, St Lucia, Queensland: University of Queensland Press.

Anderson, J. (1982a). 'Cue systems, cohesion and comprehending', *Australian Journal of Remedial Education*, 14: 56–9.

Anderson, J. (1982b). 'The measurement of the perception of cohesion: a second language example'. Paper presented at the Ninth World Congress on Reading, Dublin.

Anderson, J. (1983). 'The writer, the reader and the text'. In B. Gillham (ed.) *Reading Through the Curriculum*, London: Heinemann Educational Books, pp. 82–94.

Anderson, R.C., Spiro, R.J. and Anderson, M.C. (1977). *Schemata as Scaffolding for the Representation of Information in Connected Discourse*. Technical Report No. 24, Urbana, University of Illinois: Center for the Study of Reading.

Applebee, A.N. (1978). *The Child's Concept of Story*, London: The University of Chicago Press.

Bailey, V. and Wise, E. (1971). *Focus on History: The Early Stuarts*, London: Longman, pp. 28–9.

Baumann, J.F. (1986/87). 'Teaching third grade students to comprehend anaphoric relationships: The application of a direct instruction model', *Reading Research Quarterly*, XXI(1): 70–90.

Baumann, J.F. and Stevenson, J.A. (1986). 'Teaching students to comprehend anaphoric relations'. In J.W. Irwin (ed.) *Understanding and Teaching Cohesion Comprehension*, Newark, Delaware: International Reading Association, pp. 95–123.

de Beaugrande, R.–A. and Dressler, W.U. (1981). *Introduction to Text Linguistics*, London: Longman.

de Beaugrande, R.-A. (n.d.). *Design Criteria for Process Models of Reading*. English Department Technical Report NL–8, Gainesville: University of Florida (unpublished observations).

Bissex, G.L. (1980). *Gnys at Work: A Child Learns to Read and Write*, Cambridge, MA: Harvard University Press.

Blank, M., Rose, S.A. and Berlin, L.J. (1978). *Pre-school Language Assessment Instrument*, New York: Grune and Stratton.

Blank, M. and Milewski, J. (n.d.). 'Coding manual for dialogue with pre-schoolers: a cognitively based system of assessment (unpublished observations).

Bormuth, J.R., Carr, J., Manning, J. and Pearson P.D. (1970). 'Children's comprehension of between and within sentence syntactic structures', *Journal of Educational Psychology*, 61: 349–57.

Brimer, M.A. and Dunn, L.M. (1962). *English Picture Vocabulary Test*, Bristol: Educational Evaluation Enterprises.

Brown, R. (1973) *A First Language: The Early Stages*, London: George Allen and Unwin.

Brown, R. and Bellugi, U. (1964). 'Three processes in the child's acquisition of syntax', *Harvard Educational Review*, 34(2): 133–51.

Bruner, J. (1982). 'Reading for signs of life: a review of Bettleheim and Zelan "On learning to read" ', *New York Review of Books*, 1 April: 19–20.

Bryant, P. and Bradley, L. (1985). *Children's Reading Problems*, Oxford: Basil Blackwell.

Cairney, T.H. (1990). *Teaching Reading Comprehension*, Milton Keynes: Open University Press.

Campbell, R. (1991). *Reading Together*, Milton Keynes: Open University Press.

Campbell, R. and Wales, R. (1970). 'The study of language acquisition'. In J. Lyons (ed.) *New Horizons in Linguistics*, Harmondsworth: Penguin, pp. 242–60.

Carpenter, P.A. and Just, M.A. (1977a). 'Integrative processes in comprehension'. In D. La Berge and S.J. Samuels (eds) *Basic Processes in Reading: Perception and Comprehension*, Hillsdale, NJ: Lawrence Erlbaum Associates, pp. 217–41.

Carpenter, P.A. and Just, M.A. (1977b). 'Reading comprehension as eyes see it'. In M.A. Just and P.A. Carpenter (eds) *Cognitive Processes in Comprehension*, Hillsdale: Lawrence Erlbaum Associates, pp. 109–40.

Cazden, C.B. (1983). 'Play with language and metalinguistic awareness: one dimension of language experience'. In M. Donaldson *et al.* (eds) *Early Childhood Development and Education*, Oxford: Blackwell.

Chai, D.T. (1967). *Communication of Pronominal Referents in Ambiguous English Sentences for Children and Adults.* Report No. 13, Ann Arbor, Michigan: Center for Human Growth, ERIC document, ED 012 889.

Chapman, L.J. (1983a). *Reading Development and Cohesion,* London: Heinemann Educational Books.

Chapman, L.J. (1983b). 'A study in reading development: a comparison of the ability of 8-, 10- and 13-year old children to perceive cohesion in their school texts'. In B. Gillham (ed.) *Reading Through The Curriculum,* London: Heinemann Educational Books, pp. 165–78.

Chapman, L.J. (1984). 'Nurturing every child's literacy development: a four-pronged teaching strategy'. In D. Dennis (ed.) *Reading: Meeting Children's Special Needs,* London: Heinemann Educational Books, pp. 54-65.

Chapman, L.J. (1987). *Reading: From 5–11 years,* Milton Keynes: Open University Press.

Chapman, L.J. and Anderson, E. (1982). 'Children's perception of textual cohesion'. In K. Tuunainen and A. Chiaroni (eds) *Full Participation,* Joensuu, Finland: The University of Joensuu, pp. 139–56.

Chomsky, N. (1957). *Syntactic Structures,* The Hague: Mouton.

Chomsky, N. (1959). 'Review of *Verbal Behaviour* by B.F. Skinner', *Language,* 35: 26–58.

Chomsky, N. (1965). *Aspects of the Theory of Syntax,* Cambridge, MA: MIT Press.

Clark, M.M. (1976). *Young Fluent Readers,* London: Heinemann Educational Books.

Clark, M.M., Barr, J. and Dewhirst, W. (1985). *Early Education of Children with Communication Problems: Particularly Those from Ethnic Minorities.* Report of a DES research project, Educational Review, University of Birmingham, Offset Publication Number 3.

Clay, M.M. (1972). *Reading: The Patterning of Complex Behaviour,* London: Heinemann Educational Books.

Coulon, R. (1983). 'Discourse analysis and the reading of specialist foreign language texts'. Paper presented at the Hatfield (BAAL) Conference on Discourse Structure.

Davies, F. and Greene, T. (1984). *Reading for Learning in the Sciences,* Edinburgh, Oliver and Boyd.

Davis, C. and Stubbs, R. (1988). *Shared Reading in Practice,* Milton Keynes: Open University Press.

Department of Education and Science (1975). *A Language for Life* (The Bullock Report), London: HMSO.

Department of Education and Science (1988). *Report of the Committee of Inquiry into the Teaching of English Language* (The Kingman Report), London: HMSO.

Department of Education and Science and The Welsh Office (1990). *English in the National Curriculum No. 2,* London: HMSO.

van Dijk, T.A. (1977a). *Text and Context,* London: Longman.

van Dijk, T.A. (1977b). 'Semantic macro-structures and knowledge frames in discourse comprehension'. In M.A. Just and P.A. Carpenter (eds) *Cognitive Processes in Comprehension,* Hillsdale, NJ: Lawrence Erlbaum Associates, pp. 3–32.

Donaldson, M. (1978). *Children's Minds,* Glasgow: Collins/Fontana.

Donaldson, M., Grieve, R. and Pratt, C. (eds) (1983). *Early Childhood Development and Education: Readings in Psychology*, Oxford: Basil Blackwell.

Downing, J. (1979). *Reading and Reasoning*, Edinburgh: Chambers.

Eden, J.E. (1991). 'Helping pupils to read for information', *Reading*, 25(2): 8–12.

Enkvist, N.–E. (1964). 'On defining style: an essay on applied linguistics'. In N.–E. Enkvist, J. Spencer and M.J. Gregory *Linguistics and Style*, Oxford: Oxford University Press, pp. 3–56.

Enkvist, N.–E. (1981). 'Review of Halliday and Hasan 1976 *Cohesion in English*, and 1980 *Text and Context: Aspects of Language in a Social Semiotic Perspective*' (unpublished observations).

Ferreiro, E. and Teberosky, A. (1982). *Literacy Before Schooling*, London: Heinemann Educational Books.

Ferreiro, E. (1985). 'The relationship between oral and written language: The children's viewpoints'. In M.M. Clark (ed.) *New Directions in the Study of Reading*, London: The Falmer Press, pp. 83–94.

Fredericksen, C.H. (1977). 'Structure and process in discourse production and comprehension'. In M.A. Just and P.A. Carpenter (eds) *Cognitive Processes in Comprehension*, Hillsdale, N.J.: Lawrence Erlbaum Associates, pp. 313–32.

Fyfe, R. and Mitchell, E. (1985). *Reading Strategies and Their Assessment*, Windsor: NFER Nelson.

Fyfe, R. and Mitchell, E. (1988). 'Assessing inquiry reading'. In C. Anderson (ed.) *Reading: The a b c and Beyond*, Basingstoke: Macmillan Educational, pp. 138–48.

Gardner, P.L. (1977). *Logical Connectives in Science*. Report to the Education Research and Development Committee, Monash University.

Gardner, P.L. (1983). 'Students' difficulties with logical connectives', *Australian Journal of Reading*, 6(1): 12–18.

Gawith, G. (1987). *Library Alive*, London: A. & C. Black.

Gerot, L. (1983). *Reading Comprehension and the Systemic–Functional Model of Language*. Mimeo, Sydney: Macquarie University.

Gibson, E. and Levin, H. (1975). *The Psychology of Reading*, Cambridge: MA: MIT Press.

Goelman, H., Oberg, A. and Smith, F. (eds) (1984). *Awakening to Literacy*, London: Heinemann Educational Books.

Good, M. and Holmes, J. (1978). *How's It Going? An Alternative to Testing Students in Adult Literacy*, London: Adult Literacy Unit.

Goodman, K.S. (1968). *The Psycholinguistic Nature of the Reading Process*, Detroit: Wayne State University Press.

Goodman, K.S. (1969). 'Analysis of oral reading miscues: applied psycholinguistics', *Reading Research Quarterly*, 5: 9–30.

Goodman, K.S. (1970). 'Reading a psycholinguistic guessing game'. In D.V. Gunderson (ed.) *Language and Reading: An Interdisciplinary Approach*, Washington DC: Center for Applied Linguistics, pp. 107–19; first printed in *Journal of the Reading Specialist*, 4:126–35 (1967).

Goodman, K.S. (1982). *Workshop session at the U.K.R.A. Annual Course and Conference*, Newcastle: Newcastle-upon-Tyne Polytechnic.

Goodman, K.S. and Gespass, S. (1983). *Text Features as They Relate to Miscues: Pronouns.* Research Report No. 7 Program in Language and Literacy, Tucson, University of Arizona: Arizona Center for Research and Development, March.

Goodman, Y. (1984). 'Initial literacy'. In H. Goelman, A. Oberg and F. Smith, (eds) *Awakening to Literacy,* London: Heinemann.

Gordon, C.G. (1980). *The Effects of Instruction in Metacomprehension and Inferencing on Children's Comprehension Abilities.* Unpublished PhD dissertation, University of Minnesota, *Dissertation Abstracts International,* 41, 3, 1004–A.

Gough, P.B. (1972). 'One second of reading'. In J.F. Kavanagh and I.G. Mattingly (eds) *Language by Ear and by Eye,* Cambridge, MA: MIT Press, pp. 331–58.

Gray, W.S. (1960). 'The major aspects of reading'. In H.M. Robinson (ed.) *Sequential Development of Reading Abilities,* Supplementary Monographs, No. 90, Chicago: University of Chicago Press.

Grieve, R. and Hughes, M. (eds) (1990). *Understanding Children,* Oxford: Basil Blackwell.

Guthrie, J.T., Seifert, M. and Mosberg, L. (1983). 'Research synthesis in reading: Topics, audiences and citation rates', *Reading Research Quarterly,* XIX(1): 16–27.

Hadley, I.L. (1985). *Perception of Anaphoric Personal Reference Items in Continuous Text, by Primary School Readers at Three Year Levels.* Unpublished MEd dissertation, The Flinders University of South Australia.

Halliday, M.A.K. (1974). *Language and Social Man* (Schools Council Programme in Linguistics and English Teaching Papers), Series 11, 3, London: Longman.

Halliday, M.A.K. (1975). *Learning How to Mean,* London: Edward Arnold.

Halliday, M.A.K. (1978). *Language as Social Semiotic,* London: Edward Arnold.

Halliday, M.A.K. (1985). *An Introduction to Functional Grammar,* London: Edward Arnold.

Halliday, M.A.K. and Hasan, R. (1976). *Cohesion in English,* London: Longman.

Halliday, M.A.K. and Hasan, R. (1980). *Text and Context: Aspects of Language in a Social–semiotic perspective,* Sophia Linguistica Working Papers in Linguistics, No. 6, Tokyo.

Hansen, J. (1981).'The effects of inference training and practice on young children's reading comprehension', *Reading Research Quarterly,* 16: 391–417.

Harrison, C. (1980). *Readability in the Classroom,* Cambridge: Cambridge University Press.

Harste, J. (1982). 'Research in context: where theory and practice meet', *Australian Journal of Reading,* 5(3) August: 110–19.

Hymes, D. (1968). 'On communicative competence'. Revised version of a paper given at Ferkauf Graduate School, Yeshiva University, 1966, excerpts published in J.B. Pride and J. Holmes (eds) (1972) *Sociolinguistics,* Harmondsworth: Penguin, pp. 269–93.

Jansen, M. (1982). In K. Tuunainen and A. Chiaoni (eds) *Full Participation: Proceedings of the Second European Conference on Reading,* Joensuu, Finland: University of Joensuu.

Johnston, P. and Pearson, P.D. (1982). *Prior Knowledge, Connectivity and the Assessment of Reading Comprehension.* Technical Report No. 245, University of Illinois at Urbana: Centre for the Study of Reading.

Jones, M. (1990). 'Children's writing'. In R. Grieve and M. Hughes (eds) *Understanding Children*, Oxford: Basil Blackwell, pp. 94–120.

Kintsch, W. (1977). 'On comprehending stories'. In M.A. Just and P.A. Carpenter (eds) *Cognitive Processes in Comprehension*, Hillsdale, NJ: Lawrence Erlbaum Associates, pp. 33–62.

Kintsch, W. and van Dijk, T.A. (1978). 'Toward a model of text comprehension and production', *Psychological Review*, 85: 363–94.

Kolers, P.A. (1968). 'Reading temporally and spatially transformed text'. In K.S. Goodman (ed.) *The Psycholinguistic Nature of the Reading Process*, Detroit: Wayne State University Press, pp. 27–40.

Kolers, P.A. (1972). 'Some problems of classification'. In J.F. Kavanagh and I.G. Mattingly (eds) *Language by Ear and by Eye*, Cambridge, MA: MIT Press, pp. 193–202.

Kolers, P.A. (1973). 'Three stages of reading'. In F. Smith (ed.) *Psycholinguistics and Reading*, New York: Holt, Rinehart and Winston, pp. 28–49.

Leonardi, M.F. (1981). 'Paragraph reading and sentence connection in achieving comprehension in English as a second language'. In L.J. Chapman (ed.) *The Reader and the Text*, London: Heinemann Educational, pp. 163–71.

Lesgold, A.M. (1974). 'Variability in children's comprehension of syntactic structures', *Journal of Educational Psychology*, 66: 333–8.

Lewis, K. and Harrison, C. (1988). 'Do young readers find direct speech difficult to read?' *Reading*, 22(1): 51–60.

Littlefair, A.B. (1991). *Reading All Types of Writing: The Importance of Genre and Register for Reading Development*, Milton Keynes: Open University Press.

Lunzer, E.A. (1976). 'The effective use of reading'. In A. Cashdan (ed.) *The Content of Reading*, London: Ward Lock Educational, pp. 151–60.

Lunzer, E.A. and Gardner, K. (1979). *The Effective Use of Reading*, London: Heinemann Educational Books.

McNeill, D. (1966). 'Developmental psycholinguistics'. In F. Smith and G.A. Miller (eds) *The Genesis of Language*, Cambridge, MA: MIT Press, pp. 15–84.

Malinowski, B. (1923). 'The problem of meaning in primitive languages'. Supplement 1 in G.K. Ogden and I.A. Richards (eds) *The Meaning of Meaning*, London: Routledge and Kegan Paul, pp. 451–510.

Martin, J. (1981). *Lexical Cohesion*. Mimeo, University of Sydney.

Maxwell, J. (1974). 'Towards a definition of reading', *Reading*, 8(2) June: 5–12.

Merritt, J.E. (1977). 'A question of standards'. In J. Gilliland (ed.) *Reading Research and Classroom Practice*, London: Ward Lock Educational, pp. 24–9.

Miller, G.A. (1967). *The Psychology of Communication*, Baltimore: Penguin Books Inc. (1969), first published by Basic Books.

Miller, G.A. (1972). 'Reflections on the conference'. In J.F. Kavanagh and I.G. Mattingly (eds) *Language by Ear and by Eye*, Cambridge, MA: MIT Press, pp. 373–82.

Miller, G.A. (1973). 'Some preliminaries to psycholinguistics'. In F. Smith (ed.) *Psycholinguistics and Reading*, New York: Holt, Rinehart and Winston, pp. 10–20, first published in *American Psychologist* (1965) 20: 15–20.

Moberly, P.G.C. (1980). *Elementary Children's Understanding of Relationships in Connected Discourse.* Doctoral dissertation, Northwestern University.

Moe, A.J. (1978). 'Cohesion as a factor in the comprehension of written discourse'. Paper presented at the Annual Meeting of the National Reading Conference, 28th, St Petersburgh Beach, Florida, December, ERIC no. ED 163 437.

Moe, A.J. and Irwin, J.W. (1986). 'Cohesion, coherence and comprehension'. In J.W. Irwin (ed.) *Understanding and Teaching Cohesion Comprehension,* Newark, Delaware: International Reading Association, pp. 3–8.

Morris, A. and Stewart-Dore, N.L. (1984). *Learning to Learn from Text,* Sydney: Addison Wesley.

Morris, J.M. (1979). 'New phonics for old'. In D. Thackray (ed.) *Growth in Reading,* London: Ward Lock Educational, pp. 99–110.

Morris, R. (1976) *Success and Failure in Learning to Read,* Harmondsworth: Penguin.

Moseley, C. and Moseley, D. (1977). *Language and Reading Among Underachievers,* Windsor: NFER.

Mosenthal, J.H. and Tierney, R.J. (1984). 'Commentary: cohesion: problems with talking about text', *Reading Research Quarterly,* XIX(2): 240–4.

Neisser, U. (1967). *Cognitive Psychology,* New York: Appleton–Century Crofts.

Neisser, U. (1976). *Cognition and Reliability,* San Francisco: W.H. Freeman.

Nicholson, T. (1983). ' "You get lost when you gotta blimmin watch the damn words." Another look at reading in the junior secondary school'. In B. Gillham (ed.) *Reading Through the Curriculum,* London: Heinemann Educational Books, pp. 62–71.

Nisbet, J. and Shucksmith, J. (1986). *Learning Strategies,* London: Routledge.

Nunan, D. (1983a). *Discourse Processing by First Language, Second Phase and Second Language Learners.* Unpublished PhD thesis, The Flinders University of South Australia.

Nunan, D. (1983b). 'Distance as a factor in the resolution of cohesive ties in secondary texts', *Australian Journal of Reading,* 6(1): 30–4.

Oller, J.W. (1979). *Language Tests at School,* London: Longman.

Paley, V.G. (1981). *Wally's Stories,* Cambridge, MA: Harvard University Press.

Pit Corder, S. (1974). 'Error analysis'. In J.P.B. Allen and S. Pit Corder (eds) *Techniques in Applied Linguistics: The Edinburgh Course in Applied Linguistics,* Vol. 3, London: Oxford University Press, pp. 122–54.

Pulver, C.J. (1983). *The Effects of Small Group and Computer Assisted Inference Training Programs on Fifth Grade Students' Comprehension of Implicit Causal Relationships.* Unpublished PhD thesis, Purdue University.

Pulver, C.J. (1986). 'Teaching students to understand explicit and implicit connectives'. In J.W. Irwin (ed.) *Understanding and Teaching Cohesion Comprehension,* Newark, Delaware: International Reading Association, pp. 69–82.

Reid, J.F. (1966). 'Learning to think about reading', *Educational Research,* 9(i): 56–62.

Reid, J.F. (1983). 'Into print: reading and language growth'. In M. Donaldson *et al.* (eds) *Early Childhood Development and Education,* Oxford: Basil Blackwell, pp. 151–65.

Reid, J.F. (1990). 'Children's reading'. In R. Grieve and M. Hughes (eds) *Understanding Children*, Oxford: Basil Blackwell, pp. 71–93.

Richards, J.C. (1974). *Error Analysis: Perspectives on Second Language Acquisition*, London: Longmans.

Richek, M.A. (1976/77). 'Reading comprehension of anaphoric forms in varying linguistic contexts', *Reading Research Quarterly*, XII: 145–65.

Robinson, H.A. (1977). 'Comprehension: an elusive concept'. In J. Gilliland (ed.) *Reading: Research and Classroom Practice*, London: Ward Lock Educational.

Robson, B. (1983). 'Encouraging interaction between staff and children with communication problems in pre-school units'. In M.M. Clark (ed.) *Special Educational Needs and Children Under Five*, University of Birmingham, Educational Review Occasional Publications, No. 9, pp. 12–19.

Rothery, A. (1983). 'Reading mathematical text'. In B. Gillham (ed.) *Reading Through the Curriculum*, London: Heinemann Educational Books, pp. 123–8.

Rumelhart, D.E. (1977). 'Toward an interactive model of reading'. In S. Dornic (ed.) *Attention and Performance VI*, Hillsdale, NJ: Lawrence Erlbaum Associates.

Rumelhart, D.E. and Ortony, A. (1977). 'The representation of knowledge in memory'. In R.C. Anderson, R.J. Spiro and W.E. Montague (eds) *Schooling and the Acquisition of Knowledge*, Hillsdale, NJ: Lawrence Erlbaum Associates.

Scottish Education Department (1990). *Working Paper 2 English Language 5–14*, Edinburgh: Scottish Education Department.

Skinner, B.F. (1957). *Verbal Behaviour*, New York: Appleton-Century Crofts.

Slobin, D.I. (1971). *Psycholinguistics*, Glenview, IL: Scott Foresman.

Smith, F. (1971). *Understanding Reading*, New York: Holt, Rinehart and Winston; 2nd edn, 1978; 3rd edn, 1983.

Southgate, V., Arnold, H. and Johnson, S. (1981). *Extending Beginning Reading*, London: Heinemann Educational Books.

Stanovich, K.E. (1980). 'Toward an interactive–compensatory model of individual differences in the development of reading fluency', *Reading Research Quarterly*, XVI(1): 32–71.

Stanovich, K.E. (1986). 'Matthew effects in reading: Some consequences of individual differences in the acquisition of literacy', *Reading Research Quarterly*, XXI(4): 360–407.

Steffensen, M.S. (1981). *Register, Cohesion and Cross-cultural Reading Comprehension*. Technical Report No. 220, University of Illinois at Urbana-Champaign: Center for the Study of Reading.

Swinson, J.M. (1986). 'Paired reading: a critique', *Support for Learning*, 1(2): 29–32.

Teale, W.H. (1982). 'Naturalistic inquiry, literacy and education', *Australian Journal of Reading*, 5(3) August: 107–9.

Templin, M.C. (1957). 'Certain language skills in children: their development and interrelationships'. Institute of Child Welfare Monograph 26, Minneapolis: University of Minnesota Press.

Tizard, B., Hughes, M., Pinkerton, G. and Carmichael, H. (1981). 'Adults' cognitive demands at home and at nursery school, *Journal of Child Psychology and Psychiatry*, 23(2): 1015–16.

Tizard, J., Schofield, W. and Hewison, J. (1982). 'Collaboration between teachers and parents in assisting children's reading', *British Journal of Educational Psychology*, 52(1): 1–15.

Topping, K. and Wolfendale, S. (eds) (1985). *Parental Involvement in Children's Reading*, London: Croom Helm.

Trevarthen, C. (1974). 'Conversations with a two-month old', *New Scientist*, 62: 230–3.

Tuinman, J.J. (1973/74). 'Determining the passage dependency of comprehension questions in five major tests', *Reading Research Quarterly*, 9: 206–23.

Valtin, R. (1986). 'Difficulties in learning to write and spell'. Paper presented at the eleventh World Congress on Reading, London.

Venezky, R.L. (1976). *A Theoretical and Experimental Base for Teaching Reading*, The Hague: Mouton.

Weir, Ruth (1962). *Language in the Crib*, The Hague: Mouton.

Wells, G. (1982). *Language, Learning and Education*, University of Bristol: Centre for the Study of Language and Communication.

Winchester, S. (1984). 'An experiment in teaching cohesion in expository texts to nine- to ten-year-old children'. In D. Dennis (ed.) *Reading: Meeting Children's Special Needs*, London: Heinemann Educational Books, pp. 186–200.

Wishart, E. (1987). 'Textual cohesion and effective teaching: a teaching strategy', *Reading*, 21(1): pp. 30–42.

Wood, M. (1986). *Dataset*, Plymouth: Garland Computing.

Index